MW00964849

Walking The Talk

Goranka Vukelich

Walking The Talk

Early childhood educators' beliefs, practices and professional identity

LAP LAMBERT Academic Publishing

Impressum / Imprint

Bibliografische Information der Deutschen Nationalbibliothek: Die Deutsche Nationalbibliothek verzeichnet diese Publikation in der Deutschen Nationalbibliografie; detaillierte bibliografische Daten sind im Internet über http://dnb.d-nb.de abrufbar.
Alle in diesem Buch genannten Marken und Produktnamen unterliegen warenzeichen-, marken- oder patentrechtlichem Schutz bzw. sind Warenzeichen oder eingetragene Warenzeichen der jeweiligen Inhaber. Die Wiedergabe von Marken, Produktnamen, Gebrauchsnamen, Handelsnamen, Warenbezeichnungen u.s.w. in diesem Werk berechtigt auch ohne besondere Kennzeichnung nicht zu der Annahme, dass solche Namen im Sinne der Warenzeichen- und Markenschutzgesetzgebung als frei zu betrachten wären und daher von jedermann benutzt werden dürften.

Bibliographic information published by the Deutsche Nationalbibliothek: The Deutsche Nationalbibliothek lists this publication in the Deutsche Nationalbibliografie; detailed bibliographic data are available in the Internet at http://dnb.d-nb.de.
Any brand names and product names mentioned in this book are subject to trademark, brand or patent protection and are trademarks or registered trademarks of their respective holders. The use of brand names, product names, common names, trade names, product descriptions etc. even without a particular marking in this works is in no way to be construed to mean that such names may be regarded as unrestricted in respect of trademark and brand protection legislation and could thus be used by anyone.

Coverbild / Cover image: www.ingimage.com

Verlag / Publisher:
LAP LAMBERT Academic Publishing
ist ein Imprint der / is a trademark of
OmniScriptum GmbH & Co. KG
Heinrich-Böcking-Str. 6-8, 66121 Saarbrücken, Deutschland / Germany
Email: info@lap-publishing.com

Herstellung: siehe letzte Seite /
Printed at: see last page
ISBN: 978-3-659-24763-7

Zugl. / Approved by: Montreal, Concordia University, 2013

I dedicate this book to my parents, Nikola and Nedeljka, whose commitment to education inspired me to consider this journey, and whose belief in me provided the courage to begin.

ABSTRACT

The inter-relationship of early childhood educators' curriculum beliefs, practices and professional identity

Goranka Vukelich, Ph.D.
Concordia University, 2012

Research Problem: The purpose of this study was to investigate the inter-relationship of early childhood educators' curriculum beliefs, practices and professional identity.

Research questions:

1. What are the relationships among curriculum practices, beliefs about curriculum, and professional identities in qualified early childhood educators?
2. What are educators' curriculum practices?
3. What are educators' beliefs about curriculum?
4. How do educators describe their professional identities?
5. What are the relations among educational and professional backgrounds of educators' and their self-reported beliefs about curriculum, their practices of curriculum, and their descriptions of professional identity?

Literature Review: The purpose of the literature review was to examine what is known about early childhood curriculum, early childhood curriculum practices, educators' beliefs about curriculum, and professional identity. The field of early childhood education endorses constructivist-inspired curriculum practices. However, the implementation of these practices seems to be complicated by educators' personal experiences and beliefs about curriculum, and the views they hold of themselves as professionals.

Methodology: This study utilized a mixed method research design that combined case study and observational assessment. Five educators who were qualified to work in licensed child-care centres with preschool aged children in Southwestern Ontario participated in this study. Data were gathered through the use of CLASS observation assessment tool (direct observation and assessment of educator curriculum practices), classroom photographs and collections of curriculum documents, as well as educator interviews. These data were triangulated and analyzed for emerging themes within each case and across all cases.

Results and Conclusions: This study uncovered a number of complex relationships including that educators hold a strong desire to contribute to children's learning and to be valued for that contribution; that educators hold strong constructivist-inspired beliefs about curriculum while at the same time they engaged in a number of instructivist-inspired curriculum practices in supporting children's learning; that educators' professional identity appears to be vulnerable to the influences of others; and that educators' professional identity appears to be a more persuasive guide to curriculum practices than educators' beliefs about curriculum.

The implication of this study is that if educators are to strengthen their implementation of constructivist-inspired curriculum practices they will require the development of an enhanced view of self as professional through an improved understanding of the theories and principles that define a constructivist curriculum framework; an examination of personal beliefs about children, learning, and education; and by becoming more comfortable with uncertainty. In addition, those involved in the professional education of educators must re-conceptualize their approach to engaging educators in learning. They should resist the teaching of curriculum techniques without the examination of the principles that inspire those techniques and the personal beliefs that may interface with the implementation of those techniques; examine resources for the messages they may portray about images of educators, children, and learning; and engage educators to develop their own curriculum techniques by combining knowledge of learning theories with unique characteristics of programs and the children within those programs.

The limitations of this study include a limited sample size, a limited range of participants, and a limited geographical location.

Future research could replicate this investigation in other geographical locations where educators might have attended different college programs; with educators who have greater diversity in years at which they graduated (new graduates, educators who graduated ten years ago, educators who graduated twenty years ago); and with educators who work with other age groups of children (infants, toddlers, school age children). Future research could also examine the influence of centre supervisors and other colleagues' practices and beliefs about curriculum on educators' practices and the formation of professional identity within a context of child-care centre culture and child-care center systems

Acknowledgements

I gratefully acknowledge the contributions of all those who helped me complete my study. First and foremost, I thank my dissertation supervisor, Professor Ellen Jacobs who guided me with extraordinary skill and proficiency as I navigated through the PhD process. From the very start Professor Jacobs impressed upon me the importance of meaningful learning and of rigour and quality in research. Through thoughtful and reflective guidance, she inspired me to extend my reach as she guided me with expertise and patience through the crafting of my final product. I thank my committee members, Dr. Saul Carliner, Dr. Nina Howe, and Dr. Miranda D'Amico. Dr. Carliner offered essential advice on issues of research design and data analysis that were invaluable to my process. Dr. D'Amico encouraged me as I sharpened my research questions and strengthened the connections among emerging concepts and Dr. Howe impressed upon me the importance of expressing my ideas in thoughtful and impactful ways. I thank Dr. Rosemary Reilly (External to Program) and Dr. Kathy Brophy (External Examiner) for their comments and excellent suggestions for improvements to the final submission of this dissertation.

I also thank the many family, friends, and colleagues who have encouraged and supported me over the years through this life altering journey. I especially thank my husband Allister and my son Sidney whose steadfast patience, support and unwavering belief in me enabled me to complete this process. Finally, I thank the participant educators of this study who welcomed me into their classrooms and generously shared themselves and their experiences.

Table of Contents

List of Figures

List of Tables

Chapter 1: Statement of Problem

This chapter introduces the associations among early childhood curriculum practices, curriculum beliefs of educators, and professional identities of educators. The first section, Early Childhood Curriculum Practices, presents an overview of curriculum practices in early childhood education and describes two conceptual frameworks that inspire those practices: instructivist-inspired curriculum framework, and constructivist-inspired curriculum framework. The second and third sections, Early Childhood Curriculum and Educator Beliefs, and Professional Identity in Early Childhood Education, provide an overview of literature and research that support the investigation of the inter-relationship of early childhood educators' curriculum beliefs, practices and professional identity. The next section, Purpose of the Study, includes the rationale for carrying out this study, and concludes with the research questions posed by this study.

Early Childhood Curriculum Practices

For the past several decades, the field of early childhood education has been occupied with describing curriculum practices that promote positive experiences for young children (Bennett, 2005; Dodge, 1995). In early childhood education, curriculum practices are carried out by educators in programs that are either licensed (required to follow government regulations) or unlicensed (not required to follow government regulations). In Canada, detailed specifications that determine the necessity of a program to be licensed varies from province to province. Generally, guidelines associated with this necessity include the total number of children in the program, whether or not parents are on the premises while the program is in operation, the total number of hours the program is in operation, and type of focus of the program: multi-focused (e.g., program that includes experiences such as creative arts, physical play, and cognitive games) or single focused (e.g., program that includes experiences such as gymnastics for tots, or music time, or science fun) (Beach, Friendly, Ferns, Probhu, & Forer, 2009).

Early childhood education programs that are not required to be licensed typically include programs such as family resource centers, church-run play groups, recreation programs, or family child care arrangements in the home of a non-relative with usually no more than five or six children. Early childhood programs that are required to be licensed typically include programs such as full-day child-care centers, half-day nursery schools and preschools, and supervised private home child care (Beach et al., 2009). Licensed child-care programs adhere to regulations that include detailed requirements related to the following aspects of a program: staff training and education; organization and management; allocation of space; choice of equipment and furnishings; health and nutrition; number of staff per group of children; maximum group size; description of program and curriculum (Beach et al., 2009).

Staff members working in early childhood programs are referred to by a number of titles. These titles have been known to include early childhood educator, educator, practitioner, child minder, teacher, and caregiver (Krough & Slantz, 2008). This same variety in titles has been used in the early childhood literature when referring to those who are directly working with children. This variety in titles has been identified by some as highlighting the condition that those working directly with children in early childhood programs do not have an identifiable title associated with them that is consistently recognized by society (McMullen & Alat, 2002; Woodrow, 2008). To avoid any confusion in the remainder of this study, those individuals working in early childhood programs will be referred to as educators, and those individuals working in school board elementary and secondary programs will be referred to as teachers.

In early childhood education programs, educators are responsible for the design and implementation of curriculum practices. These practices typically include all experiences, activities, and events carried out in a program, such as: how the

2

classroom physical space is arranged; how it may be re-arranged; how educators develop, implement, and evaluate learning experiences; how educators engage with children during play time; how educators support conflict situations among children; how educators engage parents in the program; and how educators document children's learning and the daily program (Goffin, 1994; Stacey, 2009).

In early childhood education, educators refer to a conceptual framework to guide their daily curriculum practices (Friendly, Doherty, & Beach, 2006). This conceptual framework outlines principles of how children develop and learn, and offers a declaration of values and philosophical tenets that steer daily curriculum practices (Jalongo, Fennimore, Pattnaik, Laverick, Brewster, & Mutuku, 2004; Kamerman, 2000). The interpretation of a conceptual framework and the eventual implementation of curriculum practices inspired by that framework is a process that is neither simple nor linear. As described by Edwards (2003), "the creation of curriculum is a human endeavour, and like all human endeavours involves the cultural values, beliefs, assumptions, theories and languages of its developers in its very construction" (Edwards, 2003, p. 251). This view is echoed by Dahlberg and her colleagues, who emphasize that early childhood curriculum is profoundly complicated and influenced by a number of variables including our personal and social constructions of children and childhood, and our views of the purpose of curriculum and of pedagogy (Dahlberg, Moss, & Pence, 2007).

In early childhood education, conceptual frameworks of curriculum fall along a continuum from instructivist-inspired curriculum framework to constructivist-inspired curriculum framework (Bennett, 2005; Katz, 1999). Educators working in early childhood classrooms are not described as being either exclusively instructivist or exclusively constructivist as they rarely engage in practices that are purely inspired by either framework (Chaille, 2008). The reality of their everyday work requires them to balance the influences of these frameworks in a way that best supports children's learning (Katz, 1999; Stacey, 2009). Engaging in practices that are informed by a

3

conceptual framework is more about having beliefs in the principles that define a framework than it is about following a set of exact practice guidelines. In her writings about early childhood settings, Christine Chaille (2008) describes the implementation of curriculum practices as a continuum founded upon beliefs of how children construct knowledge. These beliefs inspire educators to make day-to-day curriculum decisions and to engage in practices that support those beliefs (Chaille, 2008).

An instructivist-inspired curriculum framework is often referred to as didactic learning and academically-oriented practice (DeVries & Kohlberg, 1990). Rooted in theories of behaviorism and stimulated by the writings of Edward Thorndike and B. F. Skinner, an instructivist-inspired curriculum framework is emphasized by a belief that the purpose of curriculum is to meet predetermined competencies that provide learners with necessary skills for later academic achievements (Marlowe & Page, 1998; Palinscar, 1998). Such a framework gives rise to curriculum practices that focus on transmitting a decontextualized, predetermined body of knowledge from expert educator to novice learner. In early childhood settings, this predetermined body of knowledge is often organized around content themes or units that are largely made up of factual information often separate from children's interests (Crowther, 2003).

Early childhood curriculum practices inspired by predetermined themes have been described as problematic because in order to stay true to the theme, activities created by educators are often artificially engineered, resulting in shallow and misguided learning for children (Krough & Slantz, 2008). In implementing themed-based activities, educators often make use of pre-planned lessons, worksheets, and repetitive drill and practice strategies that are supplied through theme books and kits and are disconnected from children's experiences. Educators rely on reinforcement strategies to transmit knowledge to the children in their programs and to assess the children's expression of that knowledge (DeVries & Kohlberg, 1990; Goffin, 1994; Katz, 1999).

On the opposite end of the continuum, a constructivist-inspired curriculum framework is founded upon a belief that knowledge and understanding are co--

4

constructed through the social interactions that occur between learner and educator as both become actively engaged in the learning process (Phillips, 1995; Twomey-Fosnot, 1996). Based on a theory that dates back to Aristotle and the ancient Greeks, which views knowledge as a phenomenon to be constructed by the learner not instructed by the educator, constructivism offers the field of education a theory that explains the nature of knowledge and how human beings learn to inform and not prescribe curriculum practices (Boudourides, 2003; Perkins, 1999).

In early childhood education, curriculum practices inspired by a constructivist framework have been referred to as developmentally appropriate practice (DAP), child-centered curriculum, and emergent-oriented curriculum (Booth, 1997; Bredekamp & Copple, 1997; Jones & Nimmo, 1994). A constructivist-inspired curriculum framework gives rise to play-based practices that require educators to engage with children as they construct their own theories about the world around them (Chaille, 2008). These curriculum practices are built upon a foundation that views children as learners who are capable of such construction, and educators who are capable of participating as social partners in this learning journey.

Constructivist-inspired curriculum practices view learning as a work in progress that is being co-constructed by educators and children as they explore ideas, and develop and test theories through a process of social engagement (Chaille, 2008; Katz, 1999). These practices compel educators to recognize children's interests and to adopt a sense of wondering that is not limited by the absolute truths and boundaries of their own adult knowledge and experience as they create stimulating learning environments and guide children through knowledge discovery and meaning-making (Bredekamp & Copple, 1997; Curtis & Carter, 2008; DeVries & Kohlberg, 1990; Katz, 1999).

In early childhood education, a review of literature and research dedicated to the examination of curriculum practices that promote positive experiences for young children has repeatedly pointed to curriculum features characterized by a constructivist-inspired framework (Arnett, 1989; Burchinal, Peisner-Feinberg, Bryant,

5

& Clifford, 2000; Burts, Hart, Charlesworth, & Kirk, 1990; Maccoby & Lewis, 2003; Marcon, 2002; Whitebrook, Howes, & Phillips, 1990).

Research studies that have investigated the effects of constructivist- and instructivist-inspired curriculum practices have been largely comparative in nature. That is, they have compared the effects of curriculum features characterized by a constructivist-inspired framework on child development outcomes to the effects of curriculum features characterized by an instructivist-inspired framework on child development outcomes. In particular, findings from these studies have demonstrated that young children who experience constructivist-inspired curriculum practices demonstrate greater gains in language development, social and cognitive skills, higher motivation, and experience less stress than do young children who experience instructivist-inspired curriculum programs (Arnett, 1989; Burchinal et al., 2000; Burts et al., 1990; Maccoby & Lewis, 2003; Marcon, 2002; Whitebrook et al., 1990).

In the early childhood literature, many authors accept the view that a constructivist-inspired curriculum framework is the accepted norm for guiding curriculum practices that promote positive experiences for young children (Bennett, 2005; Dahlberg, Moss, & Pence, 2007; DeVries & Kohlberg, 1990; DeVries, Reese-Learned, & Morgan, 1991; Jones, Evans, Rencken, Stringer, & Williams, 2001; Katz, 1999; National Research Council, 2001). As an example, one author articulates the following argument:

> Emergent curriculum is the most sensible approach to teaching young children. Preselected, presequenced lesson plans cannot possibly offer a good fit in guiding the interactions of one classroom's unique group of people. The teacher's agenda is not static; it is dynamic, based in part on her or his evolving goals for the children, individually and collectively (Jones et al., 2001, p. 3).

In support of educators' understanding and eventual implementation of curriculum practices inspired by a constructivist framework, many post-secondary early childhood programs in North America introduce students to a constructivist-

6

inspired curriculum framework and to practices associated with this framework (Black & Ammon, 1992; Phillips & Hatch, 2000). "Most of the professional development in which preschool teachers and caregivers engage is in programs permeated with DAP-related values" (McMullen, Elicker, Goetze, et al., 2006, p. 86). In addition, professional associations, such as the National Association for the Education of Young Children (NAEYC) and the Canadian Child Care Federation (CCCF), as well as a number of early childhood experts, endorse constructivist-inspired curriculum practices (Bennett, 2005; Dahlberg et al., 2007; DeVries & Kohlberg, 1990; Jones et al., 2001; Reynolds, Wang, & Walberg, 2003; Saracho & Spodek, 2002).

In Canada, at the time of this study, four provinces (Quebec, New Brunswick, Ontario, and British Columbia) had developed provincial curriculum frameworks for child-care programs to follow, and two additional provinces (Manitoba and Prince Edward Island) were in the process of finalizing their documents (Langford, 2010). The curriculum practices promoted by each of the existing frameworks are consistent with a constructivist-inspired curriculum paradigm. Of the four provinces that have released provincial curriculum frameworks, New Brunswick has legislated that all licensed programs in the province are to implement practices associated with emergent curriculum (Whitty, 2009).

Even though constructivist-inspired curriculum practices are endorsed by many individuals and professional groups associated with the field of early childhood education, several studies have revealed that constructivist-inspired curriculum practices are not consistently implemented by educators (Phillipsen, Burchinal, Howes, & Cryer, 1997; Pianta, Howes, Burchinal, et al., 2005). This contradiction has stimulated an interest in examining factors that contribute to influencing early childhood curriculum practices. The results of these examinations reveal that educators' beliefs about children, children's learning, and curriculum exert significant

7

authority in guiding their daily curriculum practices (Bryant, Clifford, & Piesner, 1991; Cassidy, Buell, Pugh-Hoese, & Russell, 1995; Cassidy & Lawrence, 2000; Charlesworth, Hart, Burts, Thomasson, Mosley & Fleece, 1993; File & Gullo, 2002; McMullen & Alat, 2002; Vartuli, (1999); Wilcox-Herzog & Ward, 2004). "Researchers have confirmed that teacher's (educators) personal teaching beliefs and philosophies (i.e., what they think about the impact of teaching in general, as well as their understanding of how children learn) play a critical role in actual teaching practices and classroom decisions" (McMullen et al, 2006, p. 81).

Early Childhood Curriculum and Educator Beliefs

Educators' curriculum practices are profoundly influenced by a unique belief system that has been developed over a period of time through a combination of factors that includes personal experiences and professional knowledge (Charlesworth et al., 1993; 1996; Kagan, 1992; Pajares, 1992; Richardson, 2003). Personal beliefs are "psychologically held understandings, premises, propositions, about the world that are felt to be true" (Richardson, 2003, p. 2). Unlike knowledge, beliefs do not require a truth condition or acceptance by the community (Green, 1971; Nisbett & Ross, 1980). Personal beliefs contain a significant force assigned to them by the individual who holds them merely because that individual feels the beliefs to be true (Green, 1971; Nisbett & Ross, 1980). As personal beliefs have been constructed over a long period of time, they contain strength and sustainability that make them difficult to change. Even when new, contradicting evidence that challenges existing beliefs is encountered, research in education suggests that belief change in educators is difficult to achieve (File & Gullo, 2002; Nisbett & Ross, 1980; Smith, 1997; Tillema, 1995).

Green's (1971) early work on the nature of teaching may offer an explanation as to why educators' beliefs may be difficult to change. His findings suggest that beliefs are organized in the brain in clusters, and that exchanges between these clusters are minimal. This characteristic of minimal exchanges among belief clusters allows one individual to hold a series of beliefs in one cluster that may be incompatible with the series of beliefs being held in a separate belief cluster (Green, 1971). Green further explains that due to the personal nature of belief development, some personal beliefs reflect deeply held convictions about ideas that have been developed over a long period of time, making those beliefs more central than others and more difficult to shift (Green, 1971). Additional research findings in teacher education and belief change reveal that when knowledge and evidence about specific topics in education are presented to pre-service teachers, it is not uncommon for them to be selective in attending to information that confirms their pre-existing beliefs and strengthens them further contributing to the *I told you so* phenomenon (Anderson, 2001).

In a study examining the viewpoints of 119 pre-service educators, File and Gullo (2002) determined that early childhood education students involved in practice teaching held curriculum beliefs, and favoured child expectations and curriculum strategies that were in line with DAP curriculum practices while at the same time they promoted curriculum practices associated with behavior guidance that did not parallel these same practices. The opposing viewpoints held by these pre-service educators suggest that educators are capable of holding beliefs associated with curriculum practices that are incompatible with each other. The viewpoints of behavior guidance curriculum practices of these pre-service educators may have stemmed from a cluster of personal beliefs associated with social behavior and social etiquette that had been developing over a long period of time, and as suggested by Green's ideas (1971), these beliefs may have coexisted in an unrelated fashion with a cluster of beliefs associated with what they learned more recently about child development that is more consistent with DAP beliefs.

The research findings between educators' curriculum practices and their beliefs about curriculum draw attention to the complicated nature of translating recommended curriculum guidelines into practices, and the complexities of transmitting recommended curriculum frameworks through professional educator preparation. As stated earlier, in early childhood education, curriculum practices are guided by a framework of principles that reflect pedagogical values about children and about learning. This framework provides a broad outline of the processes through which children may experience learning, a process that informs not prescribes curriculum practices. As a result, the eventual implementation of early childhood curriculum practices requires educators to translate this framework and accompanying principles into specific daily practices and interactions with children (Jalongo et al., 2004; Kamerman, 2000). This process of translating curriculum frameworks into daily practices involves the filtering of those frameworks through personal beliefs. This filtering process contributes to making curriculum practices vulnerable to educators' experiences and views about children, learning, and their own professional identity.

Professional Identity in Early Childhood Education

Recently, experts in the field of early childhood education have turned their attention to investigating professional identity in association with curriculum practices (Fenech & Sumsion, 2007; Kashin, 2009; Langford, 2008; McGillivray, 2008; Moss, 2006; Nimmo & Park, 2009; Osgood, 2006a). While the investigation of professional identity is relatively new in early childhood education, it has been studied more extensively in other fields, such as nursing (Crawford, Brown, & Majomi, 2008; Fealy, 2004; Roberts, 2000) and elementary and secondary education (Beijaard, Meijer, & Verloop, 2004; Beijaard, Verloop, & Vermunt, 2000; Britzman, 1992; Day, Kington, Stobard, & Sammons, 2006).

Professional identity has been characterized as the interplay between what the professionals themselves perceive to be important in their work based on their experiences and personal backgrounds, and the influence and perceptions of other people, including broadly accepted images in society (Tickle, 2000). This interplay contributes to the image professionals have of themselves and of their profession. For early childhood educators, professional identity has been referred to as a complex paradigm influenced by individual dispositions and emotions; daily interactions and relationships; training and education; and the cultural and economic constructs of children, childhood, and those who work with children in our society (Britzman, 1992; Day et al., 2006). According to McGillivray (2008), "Professional identity is construed on shifting but simultaneously enduring perceptions, influenced by history, society, ideologies and discourse" (p. 246).

The ways in which educators view themselves are intricately connected with the ways in which the public views children and the individuals (educators) who work with children. A study conducted to assess how the public views educators revealed that their work is not highly valued and was termed as mindless, custodial work (Kagan & Cohen, 1997). With this public image being an influencing contributor to self-image, it is with little surprise that the 1998 findings from a Canadian study revealed that only 19.9% of educators surveyed reported that professionals in other fields respected their work and only 8.2% reported that the general public respected the work in which they were engaged (Doherty, Lero, Goelman, La Grange, & Tougas, 2000).

Studies in elementary teacher education suggest that the expectations and conceptions of teacher work by others not associated with teaching have the capacity to impact an individual teacher's professional identity (Reynolds, 1996). Further, the development of professional identity is contextually dependent on one's developing notions of the broader professional community that includes the institutions in which teachers find themselves (Goodson & Cole, 1994). For early childhood educators, the professional community includes the child-care centers in which educators work and the parents of the children with whom they work. In a study investigating the impact of emergent curriculum on the practice and self-image of early childhood educators, Kashin (2009) suggested that the practices and working conditions of a child-care

11

center "convey messages regarding the extent to which staff are respected" (p. 62). These messages influence opportunities for decision-making regarding various center issues including curriculum decisions (Kashin, 2009). This finding is supported by a study investigating staff turnover and recruitment challenges in child-care centers that identifies opportunities for center decision-making as a predictor of staff turnover. Specifically, findings reveal that the extent to which staff members perceive they have input into center decisions predicts the proportion of staff in a center who intend to leave within 12 months (Doherty & Forer, 2005).

McGillivray (2008) argues that the professional identity of early childhood educators is influenced by a tension between the perceptions of a workforce that is defined as caring, maternal, and gendered, and one that is defined as professional, degree educated, and highly trained. This argument is echoed by Moss (2006), who writes that society's expectations of early childhood educators is "to apply a defined set of technologies through regulated processes to produce pre-specified and measurable outcomes to meet the state's social and educational goals" (p. 35). A recent study by Nimmo and Park (2009) extends this argument by proposing that society's view of educators as low-skilled babysitters makes them vulnerable to developing professional identities whereby they perceive themselves as passive consumers of other experts' knowledge. This view can be especially problematic for educators, as implementing constructivist-inspired curriculum practices requires the embracing of action research to engage in reflective thinking for the purpose of constructing understanding to impact daily practice.

In order for educators to shed these dominant social views of what others expect of their profession, they require a positive professional image that promotes confidence in thought and action. Achieving this is not an easy task for educators as studies indicate that even when they express significant confidence in their professional knowledge and skills, they report that their capabilities and contributions are not recognized by the general public (Doherty et al., 2000; Kagan & Cohen, 1997), family, friends, or the parents of the children in their programs (Whitebrook & Sakai, 2004). Collectively, these findings highlight the complex relationship among educators' beliefs, professional identity, and classroom practices (Kagan, 1992; Moss, 2006; Nimmo & Park, 2009; Pajares, 1992), and draw specific attention to the authority of the subjective, personal element of educators' perceptions of self in translating a curriculum framework into practice.

Purpose of the Study

The purpose of this study is to examine the inter-relationship of professional identity, beliefs about curriculum, and curriculum practices of qualified early childhood educators. The main research question guiding this study is: What are the relationships among beliefs about curriculum, curriculum practices, and professional identities in qualified early childhood educators? This central research question gives rise to the following secondary questions:

1) What are qualified early childhood educators' curriculum practices?

2) What are qualified early childhood educators' self-reported beliefs about curriculum?

3) How do qualified early childhood educators describe their professional identity?

4) What are the relations among educational and professional backgrounds of qualified early childhood educators and their self-reported beliefs about curriculum, their practices of curriculum, and their descriptions of professional identity?

Chapter 2: Literature Review

The following chapter presents, in more detail, information about early childhood curriculum, educators' beliefs about curriculum, and educators' professional identity. The first section, General Overview of Early Childhood Curriculum, provides an overview of early childhood curriculum and outlines conceptual frameworks and regulatory licensing requirements in relation to curriculum practices. Specifically, this section emphasizes the instructivist and constructivist conceptual frameworks and describes the curriculum practices that are inspired by each. Additionally, this section profiles the province in Canada in which this study took place, Ontario, in explaining how licensing regulations and provincial curriculum frameworks relate to curriculum practices.

The second section, Early Childhood Curriculum Practices and Child Development Outcomes, creates the links between early childhood curriculum practices and child outcomes. The next three sections, Curriculum Beliefs and Early Childhood Education, General Overview of Professional Identity, and Professional Identity and Early Childhood Education, extend those links to include how educators' beliefs about curriculum and educators' professional identity relate to educators' curriculum practices. This chapter concludes with the section Rationale for the Present Study that outlines the reasoning and motivation for the study.

General Overview of Early Childhood Curriculum

In early childhood education, curriculum refers to the approach that is used to educate young children. This curriculum approach is a conceptual framework that includes the theoretical orientation and goals of the program, the degree of structure of the program, the equipment and materials to be used, the role of the educators and the children in the program, and all experiences carried out by the educators during the program (Goffin, 1994; Howe, Jacobs, & Fiorentino, 2000). The conceptual framework

14

of curriculum describes the theoretical orientation of the program and the philosophical tenets and values of the program, and informs the curriculum practices carried out by educators (Jalongo et al., 2004; Kamerman, 2000). Curriculum practices include the day-to-day decisions that educators make regarding how the classroom physical space is arranged; when and how it may be rearranged; the process educators follow in developing, implementing, and evaluating learning experiences; how and when educators engage with children during play time; how educators support conflict situations among children; how and when educators engage parents in the program; and how educators document children's learning and the daily program (Goffin, 1994; Stacey, 2009). Curriculum is everything.

In a global comparison of early childhood curriculum, Bennett (2005) identified two broad types of fundamental approaches to curriculum. The first of these, the competency-oriented curriculum approach, highlights a focus on the existence of a specific body of knowledge that has been developed by an expert culture for the purpose of socializing the child into that culture. This approach to early childhood curriculum gives rise to curriculum practices that concentrate on transmitting specific facts to children through instruction. The second type of curriculum approach is the integral consultative curriculum approach that recognizes the child as a complex individual and highlights the multiple aspects of child development. The integral consultative curriculum approach builds on the natural interests of the child and gives rise to curriculum practices that integrate learning concepts, such as math, science, reading, and writing into the daily experiences of the program through play.

In a similar fashion, Katz (1999) described early childhood curriculum in North America as falling along a continuum from an instructivist-inspired curriculum framework to a constructivist-inspired curriculum framework. An instructivist-inspired curriculum framework, often referred to as didactic learning and academically-oriented practice (DeVries & Kohlberg, 1990) is similar to Bennett's (2005) competency-oriented curriculum type, in that it is underpinned by a belief that the purpose of

15

curriculum is to provide children with necessary skills for later academic achievement (Katz, 1996). Focusing on a predetermined body of knowledge to be transmitted to children, the instructivist-inspired curriculum framework requires educators to carry out curriculum practices for the purpose of instructing children to learn new information (Crowther, 2003; Goffin, 1994).

Instructivist-inspired Curriculum Framework

Rooted in theories of behaviorism, an instructivist-inspired curriculum framework can be traced to the writings of Edward Thorndike and B. F. Skinner (Marlowe & Page, 1998; Palinscar, 1998). The instructivist-inspired curriculum framework is underpinned by the belief that the purpose of curriculum is to meet predetermined competencies that provide learners with necessary skills for academic achievements (Katz, 1999). Characterized by the principles that all behavior is learned, manipulated by the environment, extinguishable, and trainable, the environment is a key factor in the instructivist-inspired learning process. Within an instructivist-inspired curriculum framework, learning is understood to occur as a result of external events that cause change in the learner's behavior due to repeated experiences in a given situation (Goffin, 1994). Learning that takes place within such a framework is understood within the context of the relationship between stimuli, and responses and reinforcers, while reinforcers are used to increase or decrease a response (Goffin, 1994).

An instructivist-inspired curriculum framework assumes that there is a required body of predetermined knowledge that exists to be transmitted from expert to novice (DeVries & Kohlberg, 1990). In addition, this framework views the knowledge to be transmitted as an objective entity that is separate from the learner's current knowledge and understanding. Within a learning situation inspired by an instructivist framework, the educator is viewed as the expert who is in possession of this knowledge, and the student is viewed as the novice who is to be the recipient of the knowledge. The role of

16

the educator is to transmit this knowledge by taking the student through a carefully constructed, step-by-step, sequenced process from simple to more complex, while the role of the student is to be a passive recipient of the knowledge transmitted. In this approach, the educator is usually in command of the learning situation as motivation and reinforcement strategies are used to navigate the student through the learning process (Maehl, 2000).

Instructivism has influenced curriculum practices by providing learning experiences based on the shaping of learners' responses through modelling, demonstration, and reinforcement as prescribed knowledge is learned and requisite skills are mastered. Historically, this approach has not focused on connecting the learner's prior experiences or interests with the new knowledge to be learned in any personally meaningful ways, the retention of the knowledge over a sustained period of time, or the integration of the knowledge (Katz, 1999). Rather, instructivism has focused on curriculum practices that cover the prescribed body of knowledge and then assess the learner's expression and demonstration of that knowledge to a satisfactory level in order to move to the next grade (DeVries & Kohlberg, 1990; Goffin, 1994; Maehl, 2000; Marlowe & Page, 1998).

In early childhood education, practices inspired by an instructivist framework are perhaps best represented by the direct instruction or DISTAR curriculum approach developed by Bereiter and Engelmann in the early sixties (Goffin, 1994; Katz, 1996). Within this approach, the purpose of curriculum is to provide children with necessary skills required for later academic achievement. Curriculum is comprised of a set of predetermined facts decided to be of importance by the adult, and the child is seen as being largely dependent on the adult's knowledge. These facts to be transmitted are largely separate from the children's interests, and are often presented through a series of pre-planned lessons using motivation and reinforcement strategies. The DISTAR curriculum approach paved the way for task-oriented drill and practice strategies that

17

used methods such as worksheets to introduce and reinforce concepts to children (Crowther, 2003; Goffin, 1994; Katz, 1999).

A theme-based approach to curriculum planning, a very popular approach in early childhood curriculum, has also been associated with instructivist-inspired learning principles (Katz, 1999; Krough & Slantz, 2008). Through this approach, educators generally select a theme, either dictated by the calendar, such as Thanksgiving or fall (Kashin, 2009), or dictated by an interest they detect through children's play, such as trucks or insects (Krough & Slantz, 2008), which becomes the focus of learning for the entire group of children for one week at a time. Educators pre-plan a series of activities around this theme for the purpose of presenting facts they determine would be of interest to children, and they determine would be of benefit to children's later academic achievements. These activities include drill and practice opportunities that focus on targeted academic skills such as letter and number recognition through memorizing lists or symbols, responding to questions or expressing tasks that can be assessed as right or wrong (Katz, 1999). While play opportunities are made available to children in the theme approach, these opportunities are not intentionally connected with strengthening concepts and deepening learning that may emerge from this play. Rather they are often treated as time fillers for children to do something while educators are preparing for learning activities, or as rewards offered that children can engage in after the learning activity has been completed. This instructivist-inspired approach to curriculum practices results in a superficial study of topics as the activities carried out typically rely on externally imposed, educator-determined goals and objectives to direct the flow of learning. This approach has been reported as restraining children's contributions and active involvement in learning as well as limiting children's integration of concept development across the curriculum (Crowther, 2003; Jalongo & Isenberg, 2000; Vartuli & Rohs, 2006).

Constructivist-inspired Curriculum Framework

At the opposite end of the curriculum continuum described by Katz (1999) is the constructivist-inspired curriculum framework. The constructivist-inspired curriculum framework is founded on a theory whose roots date back to Aristotle and the ancient Greeks, a theory of constructivism (Boudourides, 2003). Numerous philosophers, psychologists, and epistemologists have written about constructivism, its meaning, implications, and applications (Boudourides, 2003; Perkins, 1999; Phillips, 1995; Twomey-Fosnot, 1996). At its basis, constructivism is a theory of knowledge and learning that informs curriculum practices by offering an explanation regarding the nature of knowledge and how human beings learn (Twomey-Fosnot, 1996). Duckworth's (1987) succinct definition of constructivism, "meaning is not given to us in our encounters, but it is given by us, constructed by us, each in our own way, according to how our understanding is currently organized" (p. 112), provides a suitable starting point from which principles that characterize constructivism can be explored.

The constructivist-inspired curriculum framework is underpinned by the belief that knowledge and understanding are co-constructed through the social interaction between the educator and the learner as both become actively involved and engaged in the learning process. Within this framework, educators are viewed as guides of the learning process who do not have full, predetermined knowledge of all that is to be learned or in which direction the learning process may go. Within this framework, learners are viewed as capable individuals who contribute to the learning process by combining new information and ideas with what they already know and believe (Brooks & Brooks, 1999; Doolittle & Camp, 1999; Phillips, 1995; Twomey-Fosnot, 1996).

In summarizing her extensive work in the area of constructivist-inspired curriculum frameworks, Twomey-Fosnot (1996) emphasizes the importance of recognizing that a constructivist-inspired curriculum framework views learning and development as interconnected processes that influence each other and that are dependent upon each other. Twomey-Fosnot (1996) stresses that learning does

19

not occur only after development takes place, but rather that learners develop through the learning process as they actively participate in producing questions and hypothesis and test them using self-generated ideas and methods. She further emphasizes the changing nature of development and suggests that concepts acquired about objects, people, events, or transformations are usually not static, but will undoubtedly change as learners encounter new information through additional experiences. The making of mistakes is a salient feature of a constructivist-inspired curriculum framework and should not be viewed as a negative experience to be minimized or entirely eliminated. Rather, mistakes have beneficial elements that can be explored and discussed, because they have the potential to illuminate the process of understanding and strengthen personal meaning making (Twomey-Fosnot, 1996).

Collaborative learning and personal meaning making are two additional significant features of a constructivist-inspired framework (Brooks & Grennon-Brooks, 1999; Twomey-Fosnot, 1996). Collaborative learning emphasizes the idea that a classroom is a community of social discourse where all participants, students, and educators alike are learners who participate in the process of co-construction of knowledge. In such an environment, learners make their ideas public and actively initiate, defend, and communicate ideas, thereby constructing their own knowledge and contributing to the construction of others' knowledge creation. Personal meaning making refers to the idea that in order for knowledge to be relevant for the learner, it should be connected to the learner's personal frame of reference. Twomey-Fosnot (1996) stresses that all learners come to the learning situation with prior knowledge and experience and, in order to strengthen knowledge relevance, learners need to actively participate in a process of personal meaning making. They need opportunities for organizing and connecting new experiences to existing knowledge and experiences.

As educators who have written extensively about constructivist education, Brooks and Grennon-Brooks (1999) emphasize the importance of valuing learners' prior knowledge, experiences, and points of view as central features of a constructivist-inspired curriculum framework. The recognition of these features can provide relevant contributions to the learning process that can strengthen learner engagement and promotion of personal meaning making. Educators who are inspired by a constructivist framework are encouraged to structure classroom experiences to build on learners' prior knowledge, and challenge suppositions through active involvement and purposeful inquiry (Brooks & Brooks, 1999; Doolittle & Camp, 1999).

In the field of early childhood education, the constructivist framework has inspired the curriculum approaches of DAP and child-centered curriculum (Bredekamp & Copple, 1997; Jones & Nimmo, 1994), emergent-oriented curriculum (Booth, 1997; Sheerer, Dettore, & Cyphers, 1996), Creative Curriculum (Dodge, 1988), High/Scope Approach, (Hohmann & Weikart, 2002), Reggio Approach (Hendrick, 1997), and Project Approach (Katz & Chard, 2000). These approaches have in common a focus on play-based learning, building on prior interests and experiences, the importance of meaningful learning, a view of educators as co-learners, and the recognition of children as capable learners (Bredekamp & Copple, 1997; DeVries & Kohlberg, 1990; Saracho & Spodek, 2002).

Drawing upon the ideas of Jean Piaget, Lev Vygotsky, John Dewey, Jerome Bruner, and Loris Malguzzi, constructivist-inspired curriculum approaches have popularized and legitimized curriculum practices that view young children as capable learners who construct knowledge about their physical and social world through active engagements with their environment, and through social interactions each other and with educators. Educators who engage in curriculum practices inspired by a constructivist framework recognize that curriculum is constantly developing and emerging out of the numerous experiences and ideas that the children in their programs and they have. These

21

experiences and ideas emerge in a complicated web-like fashion as they give rise to additional experiences and ideas that build on each other and evolve over time.

Guided by the view that children are a valuable source for curriculum and that there is much to learn from children, educators devote considerable time to listening and observing children's interests and competencies and in recording those observations to inform themselves about curriculum directions (Chaille, 2008; Stacey, 2009). Educators inspired by a constructivist framework emphasize the complex nature of concept development through play over rote learning and reproduction of facts through group instruction (Chaille, 2008; Katz, 1999). These educators guide children through discovery and meaning making by using carefully selected questions that reach beyond the reproducing of facts and the reporting of obvious features, provocations that challenge children to go a step further in their investigation, and thoughtful suggestions that build on children's current ideas and understandings.

Through play, constructivist-inspired curriculum practices invite educators into the learning process with children not as adult experts who know the answers, but as authentic learners who are eager to learn alongside children. Through this social co-construction of knowledge, children and educators deepen their understandings of the world around them, of themselves, and of each other (Curtis & Carter, 2008; Stacey, 2009). Through this social co-construction of knowledge, children and educators express their ideas and concepts within the classroom community, making their learning visible and their voices heard. Through the use of graphic documentations (such as drawings, photographs, text, and three-dimensional representations) educators engage children in a process of expressing their learning stories, "enabling educators and children to revisit the work, reflect upon it, and uncover meaning and future directions" (Stacey, 2009, p. 20). These curriculum practices contribute to strengthening children's understanding and to the emergence of new curriculum ideas.

Individuals working in early childhood classrooms are not described as being either an instructivist or a constructivist educator as they rarely engage in practices that

22

are purely inspired by either framework (Chaille, 2008). The reality of their everyday work requires them to balance the influences of these frameworks in a way that best supports children's learning (Katz, 1999; Stacey, 2009). Engaging in practices that are informed by a constructivist framework is more about having a belief in the principles that define constructivism than it is about following a set of exact practice guidelines. In her writings about constructivism in early childhood settings, Christine Chaille (2008) describes the implementation of constructivist practices as a continuum founded on a belief that children construct knowledge. This belief inspires educators to make curriculum decisions and to engage in practices that support it (Chaille, 2008).

Provincial Curriculum Frameworks

The Organization for Economic Co-operation and Development (OECD) recommended that countries create a national quality framework for early childhood services that includes the following:

> A statement of the values and goals that should guide early childhood centers to facilitate development and learning; an outline of the knowledge, skills, dispositions and values that children at different ages can be expected to master across broad developmental areas; and pedagogical guidelines outlining the process through which children achieve these goals, and how educators should support them (OECD Directorate for Education, 2004, p. 11).

Following this recommendation, efforts to stimulate a national conversation in Canada for the purpose of creating a national framework were unsuccessful (Friendly, Doherty & Beach, 2006), however, a number of individual provinces (Quebec, Ontario, New Brunswick, British Columbia, Manitoba, Prince Edward Island) proceeded to develop a provincial curriculum framework (Langford, 2010). At the time of this study, all but two provinces (Manitoba, Prince Edward Island) had released those frameworks.

In 2006, the Ontario Minister of Children and Youth Services invited a group of experts to create a provincial curriculum framework that would be flexible so that it

23

could be adapted at an individual program level while still being in harmony with a broad vision, beliefs, values, and principles. Ontario created and released the curriculum framework, Early Learning for Every Child Today (ELECT), in 2006 (Ministry of Children and Youth Services, 2006). As an accumulation of early childhood curriculum and pedagogy, research findings, and the collective knowledge of early childhood experts, the Ontario curriculum framework ELECT provides research evidence, accompanying strategies, a glossary of terms, and the following values and principles to inspire educators' practices:

> Early child development sets the foundation for lifelong learning, behavior and health; partnerships with families and communities strengthen the ability of early childhood settings to meet the needs of young children; respect for diversity, equity, and inclusion are prerequisites for honouring children's rights, optimal development, and learning; a planned curriculum supports early learning; play is a means to early learning that capitalizes on children's natural curiosity and exuberance; knowledgeable, responsive early childhood professionals are essential (Ministry of Children and Youth Services, 2006, p. 8-19).

ELECT has been widely distributed to early childhood settings within the province of Ontario and has received considerable attention during the last six years. The Ontario Ministry of Child and Youth Services engaged in a campaign to support the implementation of this framework in early childhood settings. This campaign has included the availability of the document to every licensed child-care center in the province, and the financial support of professional development activities to introduce the curriculum framework to practicing educators through workshops and conferences. In addition, post-secondary early childhood education programs have been encouraged to introduce the ELECT document to students during their course of study.

This curriculum framework provides broad guidelines intended to inform, not impose practice, and is purposefully designed to invite educators to "shift from

24

prescribed, programmed curriculum to co-constructed curriculum based on negotiated beliefs, values, and principles related to early learning" (Whitty, 2009, p. 30). The absence of precise instructions as to how to translate this framework into curriculum practices contributes to a condition where educators' life experiences, understanding of curriculum, and evolving beliefs intersect to influence daily curriculum practices.

Regulations and Early Childhood Curriculum

In licensed early childhood programs in Canada, curriculum practices are influenced by conceptual frameworks of curriculum as well as by licensing regulations set out by provincial governments (Beach et al, 2009). In Ontario specifically, the provincial regulations that relate to curriculum practices are stated in the following broad terms:

Play equipment and furnishings must be of such a type and design as to meet the needs of the enrolled children in regard to their developmental stages, age, and the type of program offered. Play equipment must include equipment for gross motor activity and fine motor activity as well as provide opportunities for investigation and social interactions (*Day Nurseries Act*, R.S.O., 1990).

A daily program plan of activities and experiences must be posted and available at all times to any parent of an enrolled child. Any variation of the daily program plan must be noted in a written record kept for this purpose. The daily program plan of activities must be varied and flexible. It must include the following: activities appropriate for the development levels of the enrolled children, group and individual activities; activities designed to promote gross and fine motor skills, language and cognitive, social and emotional development; active and quiet play; some activities that are offered for several days to allow all children the opportunity to explore and participate; consideration for the varied ages within the group and the needs of the individual child; and a balance between opportunities for creative exploration and structure (*Day Nurseries Act*, R.S.O., 1990).

While these regulatory conditions provide educators with flexibility as to how they are translated into curriculum practices, as regulations, these conditions must be visible if programs are to maintain their licenses.

Associations of Early Childhood Curriculum Practices and Child Development Outcomes

In early childhood education, the investigation of curriculum practices that provide young children with positive learning experiences has largely been carried out through a lens of child development outcomes; that is, the effects of curriculum features have been examined in association with child development outcomes (Arnett, 1989; Burchinal et al., 2000; Maccoby & Lewis, 2003; Marcon, 2002; Whitebrook et al., 1990).

As early as 1942, Gardner conducted a study that compared the effects on child development outcomes of curriculum practices within nursery school programs with distinctly different curriculum approaches: one that followed a constructivist-inspired curriculum framework through play-based, child-initiated curriculum practices and the other that followed an instructivist-inspired curriculum framework through academic-based, educator-initiated curriculum practices. The results of Gardner's study demonstrated that children who attended the play-based nursery school program where educators emphasized curriculum practices that supported creativity and spontaneous play as initiated by children experienced greater social and language skill development than did children who attended the academic-based nursery school program where educators emphasized practices that highlighted the development of academic skills through direct instruction (Gardner, 1942).

A significant number of follow-up studies conducted in early childhood settings support Gardner's original findings of positive associations between child development outcomes and constructivist-inspired curriculum practices (Burts et al., 1990; DeVries et al., 1991; Marcon, 2002; Peisner-Feinberg, Burchinal, Clifford, Culkin, Howes, Kagan, & Yazejian, , 2001; Stipek, Feiler, Byler, Ryan, Milburn, & Salmon, 1998). The recent focus on brain research has also contributed to strengthening the association between type of learning environments and curriculum practices in early childhood programs and brain development. Specifically, curriculum practices that build on children's prior knowledge and competencies, engage children as decision-makers and active participants in the learning process, provide hands-on activities and relevant experiences, and support personal meaning making are positively associated with activating multiple areas of the brain simultaneously, and connecting new information to prior experiences in relevant, meaningful ways (Rushton & Larkin, 2001). The curriculum practices promoted by the research on brain development are practices inspired by a constructivist curriculum paradigm (DeVries et al., 1991; Katz, 1999; New, 1999).

A comprehensive study conducted by Stipek and colleagues (1998) investigated the relationship between type of early childhood experience (didactic vs. child-centered), and cognitive and motivational competence of young children. The participants of the study included 228 preschool and kindergarten children, 104 boys and 124 girls, from diverse ethnic backgrounds and social class. The children were randomly selected from 42 different classrooms that included private schools, non-profit programs, and for-profit programs.

Classroom classification type was determined as child centered (less basic skills) or didactic (more basic skills) through a combination of classroom observations. The observations upon which classrooms were classified focused on curriculum practices that reflected the degree to which basic skills activities were present (e.g., math, letters, days-of-the-week, use of commercially prepared materials, such as worksheets), the degree to which instruction was structured and teacher-directed (e.g., teachers made choices for children, large group instruction of content material, de-emphasis of learning through play), and the positive or negative social climate of the classroom (e.g.,

27

nurturing, respectful, and responsive teachers, positive or negative discipline approaches used). The children were assessed individually for general cognitive competence (e.g., puzzle solving, word knowledge, numerical memory, verbal fluency, and counting and sorting), and motivational competence (e.g., expectations for success, enjoyment of school and school-like activities, preference for challenges/risk taking, perceptions of ability, dependence, affect, persistence, and anxiety) both at the beginning and at the end of the first and second year of school.

Stipek et al. (1998) reported negative short-term and long-term effects for both cognitive competence and motivational competence for preschool children who experienced classrooms with curriculum practices classified as didactic, than for children who experienced classrooms with curriculum practices classified as child centered. Findings also reveal that while kindergarten children did experience some cognitive benefits from participating in classrooms with curriculum practices classified as didactic, they also expressed more negative affect, were more dependent, were less compliant, and were more likely to misbehave than were kindergarten children who participated in classrooms with curriculum practices classified as child centered.

Interestingly, findings from the same study indicate strong negative associations between didactic curriculum practices orientation and classroom climate for both preschool and kindergarten classrooms (r = -.78 and -.59, respectively). That is, both preschool and kindergarten classrooms where educators emphasized curriculum practices classified as didactic had a more negative social climate than did preschool and kindergarten classrooms where educators emphasized curriculum practices classified as child centered. The authors of this study suggested that cognitive learning of preschool age children may be adversely affected by the negative social climate created by curriculum practices classified as didactic (Stipek et al., 1998).

Study findings that link type of curriculum practices with classroom social climate are consistent with findings of an earlier study conducted by DeVries, Haney, and Zan (1991) that relates type of curriculum practices (i.e., direct instruction, constructivist, or

28

eclectic) with educators' enacted interpersonal understandings in kindergarten classrooms. Results from this study suggested that educators that implement curriculum practices classified as direct instruction were more likely to create negative classroom atmospheres than were educators who implement curriculum practices classified constructivist. Negative classroom atmosphere were described as classrooms where the educators were in control of social situations and where the children had limited opportunities to express their feelings and ideas, and limited opportunities for shared experiences and negotiation strategies (DeVries et al., 1991).

Worthy of note among the findings reported by Stipek and colleagues (1998) were the higher stress and anxiety ratings assigned to preschool and kindergarten children experiencing classrooms where curriculum practices were classified as didactic than stress and anxiety ratings assigned to preschool and kindergarten children experiencing classrooms where curriculum practices were classified as child centered. These findings are consistent with those from an earlier study conducted by Burts and colleagues (1990) that revealed significantly higher stress levels in kindergarten children who experienced programs that de-emphasized constructivist-inspired curriculum practices of child selected play time, group story, and educator recognition of child development and individual child uniqueness; and that emphasized instructivist-inspired curriculum practices of whole group instruction, workbook/worksheet activities, rote learning and direct teaching of discrete skills. This study also revealed that boys enrolled in programs that emphasized direct instruction curriculum practices exhibited higher levels of stress behaviors than girls enrolled in the same programs. Based on these findings, the authors of the study concluded that while direct instruction curriculum practices may be problematic for many young children, they might be especially problematic for young boys (Burts et al., 1990). These findings may contribute to clarifying why young boys experience greater challenges in early elementary school, and why a larger number of young boys are diagnosed with learning challenges than young girls, and how we could support them (Marcon, 2002).

29

A similar study investigating the impact of curriculum approaches on children's early learning in preschool programs supports the benefits of curriculum practices inspired by a constructivist framework (Marcon, 1999). Using data from teacher surveys of curriculum beliefs and curriculum practices, interviews with school district early childhood supervisors, and observations from external, independent classroom observers, the researcher classified programs into categories. The category classification was based on a variety of dimensions (e.g., scope of developmental goals, conceptions of how children learn, amount of autonomy given to the child, conception of educator's role, and provision of possibilities for learning from peers) that yielded three categories: child-centered instruction(CI) programs where educators emphasized child development and facilitated children's learning by allowing children to actively direct the focus of their learning through play; academically oriented (AD) programs where educators emphasized academics and used educator-directed activities to instruct children; and middle-of-the-road (M) programs where educators' beliefs and practices fell between the two opposing views (CI and AD) by endorsing a combined approach.

Sixty-five classrooms were randomly selected from a pool of 114 eligible classrooms that had been previously classified as CI, AD, or M. From these 65 classrooms, 721 four-year-old children were selected to participate in the study. Program classifications were not shared with educators participating in the study. Children were assessed individually during the spring of their preschool session for general adaptive behavior, communication skills, daily living skills, socialization, and motor development. In addition, educators who were blind to the knowledge of program classification filled out the school district progress report for each individual child. The scores from these progress reports were used as a comparison with the district standard preschoolers' classroom skills mastery ratings.

The results of this study indicated that children enrolled in CI programs scored higher in all areas of development when compared with children enrolled in AD and M programs. Additionally, children enrolled in CI programs also scored significantly higher than children enrolled in AD and M programs in general adaptive behavior, communication skills, and motor development (Marcon, 1999).

Marcon (1999) attributed the association between child development results and program type to the philosophical orientations of the curriculum frameworks and the curriculum practices of each program type. That is, the academic preparation emphasis of AD programs may have supported the instruction of written language, but may not have supported the generalized practice of communication skills through child-initiated activities and unstructured play that was emphasized through curriculum practices in CI programs. Likewise, motor development, especially gross motor development, an essential component of curriculum in CI programs that emphasized a philosophy of supporting all developmental domains, may not have garnered as much educator attention in AD programs.

In addition, results from the individual child progress reports demonstrated that children enrolled in CI programs showed significant mastery of overall district-expected skills, when compared with children enrolled in AD and M programs. Marcon (1999) identified this result as being especially interesting because it appears to contradict the logical expectation that academically oriented curriculum practices would better prepare children to tackle the competency-based grading system utilized by the school district. Study results appear to suggest that children enrolled in CI programs were able to master skills expected of them by experiencing curriculum practices inspired by a constructivist framework at a far greater level than their counterparts who experienced curriculum practices that emphasized the teaching of discrete skills. The author of the study attributed this difference to the fact that children enrolled in CI programs had greater opportunity to develop skills through context-specific experiences that were directed by their own interests and were more meaningful (Marcon, 1999).

Benefits to children's development from constructivist-inspired curriculum practices do not seem to be limited to short-term gains. Follow-up findings of children's skills in those children who participated in CI, AD, and M programs as preschoolers demonstrated positive associations between children's later school success and program type experienced as preschoolers (Marcon, 2002). Specifically, children who participated in CI preschool programs had significantly higher scores in areas of arithmetic, reading, language, spelling, handwriting, science, art, and health/physical education than did children who participated in AD and M preschool programs at end of Grade 3 and Grade 4 (Marcon, 2002).

Drawing on research findings that demonstrate positive associations between curriculum practices inspired by a constructivist framework and child development outcomes, many experts in the field of early childhood education have recommended the adoption and implementation of curriculum practices inspired by a constructivist framework (Bennett, 2005; DeVries & Kohlberg, 1990; Saracho & Spodek, 2002). The National Association for the Education of Young Children (NAEYC), the largest and most influential professional association representing the field of early childhood education in North America, has defined a set of curriculum standards that serve as a resource to both early childhood education programs for children from birth to age eight, as well as to post-secondary programs that produce graduates who work with young children (Bredekamp & Copple, 1997). Educators, experts, and researchers have embraced these standards, which are largely inspired by a constructivist paradigm, as representing best practices in the field of early childhood education (Hart, Burts, & Charlesworth, 1997).

Educators' Curriculum Practices and Beliefs About Curriculum

For early childhood educators, navigating the daily demands of implementing curriculum practices requires the balancing of children's needs, curriculum frameworks, understanding about curriculum, interpretations of regulations, and parents' expectations. The primary authority guiding this navigation process appears to be the unique belief system that educators hold (Kagan, 1992; Pajares, 1992; Richardson, 2003). This unique belief system is developed over time through a

32

combination of personal beliefs that are based on personal encounters and views, and professional beliefs that are based on understandings accumulated through education and literature (Charlesworth et al., 1993).

Personal beliefs are said to be "psychologically held understandings, premises, propositions, about the world that are felt to be true" (Richardson, 2003, p. 2) that do not require a truth condition accepted by the larger community (Green, 1971; Nisbett & Ross, 1980). In the case of personal beliefs, the only one who needs to be convinced of their truth is the individual who holds them. If that individual feels the belief to be true, the belief may easily be elevated to the status of knowledge and treated as such, without the added burden of having to defend its status to others (Kagan, 1992). Professional beliefs are developed over time through encounters with education, literature, and research (Charlesworth et al., 1993; Kagan, 1992). The development of a unique belief system is a complicated process as the personal and the professional merge in unique and often unpredictable ways to co-exist and influence curriculum decision-making (Kagan, 1992; Richardson, 2003).

Initial investigations of associations between educator beliefs and curriculum practices focused largely on assessing whether educators' beliefs about curriculum were consistent with DAP practices (Charlesworth et al., 1993; Kontos & Dunn, 1993; Wilcox-Herzog & Ward, 2004), and with identifying variables that contributed to DAP beliefs and DAP curriculum practices (Cassidy et al., 1995). The results of these investigations revealed inconsistencies in that findings from a significant number of studies demonstrated positive relationships among specialized post-secondary early childhood education, DAP beliefs, and DAP curriculum practices (Cassidy et al., 1995; McMullen & Alat, 2002; Snider & Fu, 1990; Stipek & Byler, 1997; Vartuli, 1999), while findings from an equally significant number of studies showed that specialized knowledge did not always influence DAP beliefs, and that explicit expression of DAP beliefs did not consistently translate into DAP curriculum practices (Bryant et al., 1991; Charlesworth et al., 1993; File, 1994; Kontos & Dunn,

33

1993; Wilcox-Herzog, 2002). These studies revealed that being exposed to constructivist-inspired curriculum practices of DAP through professional educator preparation was inconsistently associated with educators' endorsement or implementation of those same curriculum practices (Tattoo, 1998; Tillema, 1995; Zanting, Verloop, & Vermunt, 2001).

A study conducted by Wilcox-Herzog (2002) investigating the beliefs and practices of 47 educators indicated that specialized training in early childhood education guaranteed neither DAP beliefs, nor the expression of DAP curriculum practices. A multiple regression analysis of study results showed a moderately positive relationship among early childhood certification, educator involvement behaviors, and verbalization behaviors with children, as well as a moderate negative relationship among early childhood certification, sensitivity behaviors, and play style behaviors of educators.

The results of this study are consistent with those of a previous study of early childhood educators' professional beliefs and practices conducted by Kontos and Dunn (1993). Through a combination of self-reported ratings and classroom observations, the researchers uncovered that head educators who had experienced specialized early childhood training advocated beliefs only moderately consistent with DAP regardless of their classroom curriculum practices.

The inconsistency between educators' beliefs and curriculum practices was also highlighted by a study examining educators' perceptions of children's social skills and observations of educator-child interactions during free play (File, 1994). In this study, 36 educators, who had completed some college courses, (half of whom were enrolled in a major in early childhood education) filled out the Peer Relation Rating Scale (Asher, Singleton, Tinsley, & Hymel, 1979) and the Assessment of Teacher Role Scale (File, 1994) prior to classroom observations. These participants reported a high belief score regarding the role of the educator in supporting children's social development; however, a subsequent time sampling of their educator-child interactions revealed that they were largely uninvolved with children for two-thirds of their free-play time. During the time

34

that these educators were involved with children, they were six times more likely to support cognitive aspects than social aspects of the children's play, thus indicating an inconsistency between self-reported beliefs about curriculum (what they said they believed in) and observed curriculum practices (what type of practice they engaged in).

The inconsistency between DAP beliefs and DAP curriculum practices has inspired additional investigations that pointed to the influence of personal beliefs in professional decision-making. A study by Nelson (2000) examining personal and contextual factors that influence practices of educators who have had some type of formal training in early childhood education revealed that personal beliefs were a greater determinant of practice than were contextual factors such as support from colleagues and administrators. Results based on interviews and classroom observations further revealed that even under circumstances where educators self-reported to understand DAP curriculum practices, they made curriculum decisions not to implement these DAP practices indicating that they "did not personally believe in their value"(Nelson, 2000, p. 6).

An earlier study by Charlesworth and colleagues (1993) examining DAP beliefs and DAP curriculum practices of 204 kindergarten teachers using the Teachers' Beliefs Scale (Hart, Burts, Charlesworth, Fleege, Ickes, & Durland, 1990) and the Instructional Activities Scale (Hart et al., 1990) in combination with classroom observations, demonstrated a stronger correlation between self-reported inappropriate DAP beliefs and DAP curriculum practices than the correlation between self-reported DAP beliefs and DAP curriculum practices. The authors attributed the greater association between teachers' inappropriate DAP beliefs and teachers' DAP curriculum practices to the power of personal beliefs. As an extension of those ideas, these findings emphasize the uncertainty associated with shifting personal beliefs about curriculum practices through formal specialized training.

Turning their attention to the examination of predictors of DAP curriculum practices, Maxwell, McWillian, Hemmeter, Jones-Ault, and Schuster (2001) utilized a

35

combination of teacher reports and classroom observations to determine how well classroom and teacher characteristics predicted curriculum practices of 69 kindergarten through Grade 3 teachers. Their findings indicated that when combined, classroom characteristics, teacher characteristics, and teacher beliefs accounted for 42% of the variance in observed curriculum practices, with teacher beliefs contributing a statistically significant 11% of that variance. The results of this study elevated the authority of teachers' personal beliefs to the same significant level as classroom characteristics and grade among teachers' decisions regarding curriculum practices. In controlling for other factors, the results also revealed that teachers' personal beliefs predicted curriculum practices independent of their education levels. In other words, the teacher's personal beliefs played a key role in influencing the daily decisions they made regarding the implementation of their curriculum practices.

It has been postulated by a number of researchers that because personal beliefs have been constructed over a long period of time, they contain strength and sustainability that makes them difficult to shift. Even when new, contradicting evidence that challenges existing beliefs is encountered through professional training, research in education suggests that belief change is difficult to achieve (File & Gullo, 2002; Nisbett & Ross, 1980; Smith, 1997; Tillema, 1995). This characteristic of beliefs implies that educators' personal beliefs may not easily shift when educators are faced with newly encountered evidence or knowledge.

While this condition may be evidenced through research about educators' curriculum beliefs and curriculum practices, through their research Baum and King (2006) appeal to those educating the educators to explore new and unique approaches in their own post-secondary teaching to assist early childhood students in shifting their beliefs.

> This involves, in part, helping pre-service educators develop an ability to examine and identify the personal characteristics, beliefs, and attitudes that make them who they are and influence the way they think about educating and

(reflecting)

learning; thus influencing their decision-making process. To pre-service educations, this kind of self-examination may be an unfamiliar or uncomfortable process (Baum & King, 2006, p. 217).

These authors suggest that if those charged with the responsibility of educating educators hope that their students will embrace constructivist-inspired curriculum practices upon graduation, these post-secondary instructors will need to examine their own pedagogy and model constructivist-inspired curriculum practices through their own teaching. They suggest that post-secondary instructors should create emotionally and intellectually safe learning environments where early childhood education students can examine their beliefs and attitudes about children and about learning, and that post-secondary programs should focus on the education of the whole student that considers students' individual, cultural, and social needs (Baum & King, 2006). These ideas have been echoed by Langford (2008) who urges post-secondary early childhood education programs to move away from instructing early childhood education students to accept what is written in their textbooks and assist them in the construction of their own practices through an examination of the values and beliefs that underpin traditional curriculum practices.

Personal beliefs, while not always expressed by educators, act as powerful filters of newly encountered knowledge and information about curriculum practices (Kagan, 1992; Pajares, 1992; Richardson, 2003). The inconsistent research findings between educators' beliefs about curriculum and educators' curriculum practices draw attention to the role of personal beliefs in the day-to-day implementation of curriculum practices. As stated earlier, in early childhood education, curriculum practices are guided by a curriculum framework of principles that reflect pedagogical values about children and about learning. These principles provide a broad outline of the processes through which children may experience learning that inform curriculum practices. The eventual implementation of curriculum practices requires educators to translate curriculum guidelines into daily curriculum practices (Jalongo et al., 2004;

Kamerman, 2000). This translation is a complicated process that is not solely influenced by professional educator preparation (Tattoo, 1998; Tillema, 1995; Zanting, Verloop, & Vermunt, 2001), thus the role of educators' personal beliefs in this translation cannot be overlooked.

General Overview of Professional Identity

Research has identified educators' unique belief systems as playing a significant role in the shaping of curriculum practices (File & Gullo, 2002; Kagan, 1992; Maxwell et al., 2001). These unique belief systems have been described as complicated constructs that are vulnerable to a myriad of factors including individual perceptions, professional knowledge, contextual factors, and past experience (Nisbett & Ross, 1980; Pajares, 1992; Richardson, 2003). In the past decade, research in the field of early childhood education has exposed professional identity as an additional factor associated with educators' unique belief systems (Fenech & Sumsion, 2007; McGillivray, 2008; Moss, 2006).

Professional identity has been characterized as the interplay among the views that professionals hold about the importance of their work, the views that others hold about the importance of that work, and the broadly accepted images of that work in society (Tickle, 2000). "Professional identity is construed on shifting but simultaneously enduring perceptions influenced by history, society, ideologies, and discourse" (McGillivray, 2008, p. 246). It is a complex paradigm that is understood within a context of actions and beliefs of individuals and actions and beliefs of society.

While the topic of professional identity has been studied more extensively in other disciplines, it has emerged as a separate research area in the field of early childhood education within the last decade (Fenech & Sumsion, 2007; McGillivray, 2008; Moss, 2006). In order to describe some key features of professional identity, I draw on the research and literature of two comparable disciplines that have devoted considerable

38

attention to the study of this topic: nursing (Clifford, 1992; Crawford, et al., 2008; Rafferty, 1996; Roberts, 2000) and elementary and secondary teaching (Beijaard et al., 2004; Goodson & Cole, 1994; Nias, 1989; Sugrue, 1997). I begin by describing the comparable features that have contributed to my reasoning for including research and literature associated with nursing and elementary and secondary education in a study about early childhood education.

It is my belief that the elementary and secondary teaching discipline is similar to the early childhood education discipline in that both professions contribute to the learning of others (young children and elementary and secondary students). As such, the professionals working in both disciplines are involved in the design and implementation of curriculum practices and in constructing their professional identities by carrying out these practices.

It is also my belief that the nursing discipline shares some similar features with the early childhood education discipline. First, both disciplines are comprised of a largely female workforce (Crawford et al., 2008). In addition, both disciplines are part of larger fields within which there exist hierarchical structures that position each near the bottom of their respective field structures. Nurses are members of the health care field where the value of their work is overshadowed by the value of the work of other disciplines such as allied health professionals and physicians (Crawford et al, 2008), while educators are part of the education field where the value of their work is often eclipsed by the value of the work of teachers working in mandated elementary and secondary board-run schools. For early childhood educators this circumstance is shaped by the condition that all provinces throughout Canada mandate and fully fund elementary and secondary education through a tax base. As such, elementary and secondary level teachers are employees of school boards who benefit from provincially dictated and supported salaries, benefits, and working conditions. These teachers are associated with the profession of teaching, hold membership in a provincial federation or union, and are referred to as teachers, a term that is consistency valued and recognized by society.

39

On the other hand, in all provinces across Canada, early childhood education programs are offered and funded voluntarily by individual provinces (Beach et al., 2009). These programs are delivered by community organizations that are only partially funded by government grants, resulting on a heavy reliance on parent fees for their operations. In all provinces across Canada, other than in Quebec, educators' salaries, benefits, and working conditions are varied and dependent on the fiscal capacities and policies of the organizations for which they work (Beach et al., 2009). These characteristics contribute to a hierarchical structure within the field of education that may have the capacity to position the value of the work of educators below the value of the work of elementary and secondary teachers in our society.

In the nursing literature, the study of professional identity is associated with concerns of a perceived lack of recognition of nursing by society and the effects this social perception has on the professional identity of nurses (Clifford, 1992; Crawford et al., 2008; Rafferty, 1996; Salvage, 2006). Studies investigating professional identity in nursing indicate that society's perceptions of the work of nurses is characterized as work carried out by women that largely consists of emotional support (Rafferty, 1996) and dirty work that relies on skills of nurturing and care taking deemed objectionable by other health care professionals (Salvage, 2006). "Nursing is perceived by the public as a practical, feminine, mundane occupation that is subordinate to medicine" (Crawford et al., 2008, p. 1055). These characterizations contribute to the professional identity of nurses by devaluing their roles as serious members of health care teams.

In a study investigating how nurses describe their professional lives, researchers used a grounded research design methodology to conduct in-depth, semi-structured interviews with 34 mental health nurses of varying ages and genders that captured narratives of professional identity. Through a thematic analysis of these narratives, researchers uncovered several key emerging themes related to professional identity of nurse participants. The first two of these themes, a perception of being viewed by others as a non-profession, and a focus on waiting to be recognized by the public as a valuable member of the health care field, are both perceptions associated with the views of others. The third theme to emerge was that of nurses associating their professional identity with their work of meeting patients' physical and emotional needs (Crawford, et al., 2008). Findings from this study offered interesting insights as nurses' own perceptions of the value of the work they carried out appeared to be connected with their professional identities. These findings speak to the interconnected nature of the views of others, the broadly accepted social images, and the individual's own perceptions of the work being carried out in influencing professional identity.

Unlike concerns emerging from the nursing literature that associate the effects of a perceived lack of social recognition for the value of nursing work with the professional identities of nurses (Clifford, 1992; Crawford et al., 2008; Rafferty, 1996; Salvage, 2006), studies of professional identity in the elementary and secondary education literature, reveal a relationship between varying and competing perspectives of teachers' roles and teachers' self-images and professional identity (Beijaard et al., 2000; Goodson & Cole, 1994; Sugrue, 1997; Volkmann & Anderson, 1998). A thematic analysis of 22 studies investigating professional identity in education carried out between 1988 and 2000 revealed an emphasis on the self as an important aspect of professional identity development in elementary teachers (Beijaard et al., 2004).

A study conducted by Volkmann & Anderson (1998) that investigated personal and social influences on the formation of professional identity through the documentation of one beginning science teacher's experiences over a school year revealed a struggle to make sense of competing expectations. The data in the participant teacher's journal describing the formation of professional identity were analyzed for emerging themes. The analysis revealed conflicting images of the teacher's perceptions of what teaching is, with perceived expectations of others regarding how she was required to behave. Specifically, the participating teacher identified still feeling like a student herself, while being expected to act like a teacher; feeling unsure of content knowledge, while required to behave like an expert; and having a desire to care for

41

students, while being expected to be strict (Volkmann & Anderson, 1998). This struggle of navigating professional identity development has been described by Goodson and Cole (1994) who highlighted the importance of a professional community that offers opportunities for teachers to define, interpret, and redefine their individual personal and professional selves.

With a view to investigating how a teacher's professional self-image comes into being, Beijaard and colleagues (2000) conducted a study that posed the following three questions: (1) How do experienced teachers perceive their professional identity, at the time of the study and at the beginning of their careers?; (2) in view of this identity, what have been their most important learning experiences throughout their careers?; and (3) can factors be identified that influence these perceptions of their professional identity?

The participants of this study were 80 secondary school teachers from 12 schools in the southwestern part of the Netherlands. Fifty-three of the participants were male and varied in age with 26% being under 40, 44% between 40 and 50, and 30% over 50 years old. Fifty-two percent of participants had obtained their teaching credential at a university, while 33% completed their teacher training at colleges, and 51% of the participating teachers had more than 20 years teaching experience. The 80 participating teachers taught varied subjects with 40% teaching language, 33% teaching science and math, 17% teaching social studies, and 10% teaching art (Beijaard, et al., 2000).

Data were collected through a questionnaire that included background questions, items that represented their professional identity as a subject matter expert, didactical expert, or pedagogical expert, and items that represented factors influencing the development of their professional identity (e.g., context, experience, and biography). For the items that represented their professional identity, teachers were asked to distribute a total score of 100 among the categories that they perceived as a representation of their professional identity at the time of the study and for the period at the beginning of their teaching career. In addition, they were asked to clarify why they responded in the way they did and to identify their most important learning experiences throughout their careers (Beijaard et al., 2000).

Findings of the study revealed five categories that represented how teachers perceived their professional identity: subject matter expert, didactical expert, pedagogical expert, high on two aspects, and balanced between all three categories. Most of the teachers in the study perceived themselves as some combination of all three professional categories with subject matter expert and didactical expert assigned most frequently (38 participants at current perception and 53 participants at prior perception), and pedagogical expert assigned least frequently (3 participants at current perception and 2 participants at prior perception). While the reported results indicated that male teachers perceived themselves to be largely subject matter experts, and female teachers perceived themselves as balanced group teachers, no statistical data were offered to support this conclusion (Beijaard et al., 2000).

The comparison of teachers' current perceptions of their professional identity with their perceptions of professional identity at the beginning of their careers indicated a significant change for 69% of the participants. The change reflects a shift from perceiving themselves as subject matter experts at the beginning of their careers to perceiving themselves as being balanced among all three categories. This shift seems to have occurred most notably for the science and math teachers, whereas language teachers characterized themselves as balanced throughout their careers, and social studies teachers characterized themselves as subject matter experts throughout their careers (Beijaard et al., 2000). The authors of the study did not provide any reasons for these differences. While the researchers concluded that their methodology allowed the participants to represent their current perceptions of professional identity, they acknowledged the limitation of using a questionnaire to retrieve information from long-term memory.

Data results of influencing factors were analyzed using a one-way Analysis of Variance (ANOVA). No significant differences were found as teachers' perceptions of

43

their professional identity were not significantly related to contextual, experiential, or biographical factors. In their conclusion, Beijaard and colleagues (2000) maintained the theoretical basis of these categories; however, they admit that other investigative procedures should be explored in future research to address their relationships with professional identity. The absence of any of the influencing factors emerging as significant may be attributed to the absence of conflicting and competing social discourses associated with the value of being a post-secondary teacher working in a school.

Professional Identity and Early Childhood Education

A review of the literature in early childhood education reveals that professional identity is an emerging field of study that is gaining considerable attention in Australia (Fenech & Sumsion, 2007; Woodrow, 2008), England (Jones & Osgood, 2007; Manning-Morton, 2006; McGillivray, 2008; Moss, 2006; Osgood, 2006a), and the United States (Kagan & Cohen, 1997; Nimmo & Park, 2009), and limited attention in Canada (Kashin, 2009; Langford, 2008). The professional identity of early childhood educators has been described as a complex construct shaped by the inter-relationships of multiple socially constructed structures, including the public's views of children and those who work with children (Dahlberg et al., 2007; Kagan & Cohen, 1997; Moss, 2006); the tension between perceptions of a workforce defined as caring, maternal and gendered, to one defined as professional, degree educated, and highly trained (McGillivray, 2008); practices and working conditions of staff (Kashin, 2009); and individuals' responses to these factors (Day et al., 2006).

The public's view of individuals who work with children is shaped by social, cultural, and economic structures. These structures have been produced over time by dominant discourses in society of how children and early childhood programs have been conceptualized as "linked in a circular relationship with systems of power which

44

produce and sustain them" (Foucault, 1980, p. 131). Dominant social discourses inspire powerful representations and images that have the capacity to influence practices of a profession, dispositions, and qualities seen as desirable, and language used to describe job role (Fairclough, 2003).

Early childhood educators work with children who are young and who have been characterized through the literature, research, and policy over the years. These characterizations include the following: as innocent and vulnerable beings who are in need of protection from the world; reproducers of knowledge, identity, and culture waiting to be filled with socially determined information by adults to prepare them for school and for life; factors of a labor market supply that inhibit women from entering and/or returning to the workforce; scientific beings that progress through predictable stages; and recently, as co-constructors of knowledge, identity, and culture (Dahlberg et al., 2007).

The Organization for Economic Cooperation and Development (OECD) has identified the creation and expansion of early childhood programs to be an essential goal for nations that hope to compete economically in an increasingly globalized marketplace (OECD, 2001). According to the OECD (2001), early childhood programs have the capacity to enable the current population to enter the workforce, support the education and development of a new workforce, and improve a number of social problems.

Over the years, these representations of children and of early childhood programs have contributed to the public discourse of the early childhood workforce, and this discourse contributes to shaping the professional identity of the members of that workforce. A study conducted by Pacini-Ketchabaw (2005) examining regulations for child-care programs in Ontario, Day Nurseries Act Regulation 262 (DNA), reveals an emphasis on three discourses that have emerged through the document: medical supervision of children attending child-care centers; normalizing the lives of poor families through child-care centers; and child development through strict programming and behavioral guidelines of child-care centers. Each one of these discourses gives rise

45

to a particular image of the field of early childhood education as dominated by health and safety, the rescuing of those less fortunate and intervening through programs in order to normalize children's development. Each of these discourses has the capacity to influence society's image of the work of early childhood educators and to shape the professional identities of those working within the field.

One dominant image of early childhood educators in North American society is that of educator as substitute mother (McGillivray, 2008; Moss, 2006). The image of substitute mother is associated with working with young children, a segment of the population that is viewed as vulnerable, requiring a considerable amount of physical and emotional care, but not consistently perceived as requiring significant cognitive stimulation.

Historically, physical and emotional care of others has been associated with unpaid, taken-for-granted work linked with women and motherhood. This association has contributed to a social view of the early childhood workforce as maternal and unskilled, and a perception of the educator associated with that workforce as carrying out the work she was born to do without requiring any formal knowledge or training (Moss, 2006). This association is similar to the one reported in the nursing literature to devalue the work of nurses, also a largely female workforce, as it includes the provision of physical and emotional care as a component of work responsibilities (Rafferty, 1996; Salvage, 2006).

The early childhood worker as a substitute mother produces an image that is both gendered and assumes that little or no education is necessary to undertake the work which is understood as requiring qualities and competencies that are either innate to women (maternal instinct) or else are acquired through women's practice of domestic labor (housework skills) (Moss, 2006, p. 34).

The social characterization of the early childhood workforce as unskilled and maternal is echoed by research findings in a study carried out by McGillivray (2008). This study employed a discourse analysis of print resources relating to early years care and education in England between 1940 and 2003. The researcher collected textbooks, academic journals, government policy documents, and specialist magazines for early years' practitioners. These were reviewed for terminology and emerging themes that identified and described members of the early years' workforce. Findings revealed that the themes of "being maternal, being a mother, a liking for children, having good sense, being kind and loving, being warm and sensitive" (McGillivray, 2008, p. 250) were used extensively throughout the documents in describing those who work with young children. These terms contribute to the social discourses of desirable qualities required of those working with young children.

A related study that explored discourse and associations in shaping professional identity examined dominant pedagogical discourses within an urban Ontario, two-year, early childhood college preparation program (Langford, 2008). Recurrent statements and wording about the qualities, dispositions, and responsibilities of a good early childhood educator (ECE) were identified, and their use by students in shaping professional identity was documented. Data from 10 textbooks written by American and Canadian authors, six instructor interviews, and 204 student assignments collected over two years were analyzed through inductive data analysis, which generated patterns of relationships. These relationships "indicated that the discourses of the good ECE focus primarily on the personal qualities of passion, happiness, inner strength, caring, and alertness to an individual child's needs and interests" (Langford, 2008, p. 82).

While findings revealed that data from both textbooks and instructors acknowledge the undervalued salaries and working conditions of being employed in the field of early childhood education, they also impress upon "the good ECE" to find ways to cope with these unfortunate financial conditions and continue caring for young children. Langford (2008) suggests that dialogue found in textbooks and reinforced by instructors is based upon an ideology that requires female educators to fulfill the social goal of producing well-adjusted children, knowingly at a cost to their own financial success. She urges those involved in early childhood educator preparation programs to carefully consider

47

the discourses that shape classroom experiences, to critically examine the resources being used and "offer students the intellectual tools to critically evaluate their roles within various social and cultural contexts and to develop their professional identification out of their own experiences with theory and practice" (Langford, 2008, p. 97).

A second dominant image is that of the early childhood educator as technician (Fenech & Sumsion, 2007; Moss, 2006). Technicians carry out predetermined technologies that have been engineered, often through regulated processes, to produce measurable outcomes. According to Moss (2006), the image of the early childhood educator as technician is shaped by the social discourse that programs delivered in a particular way have the capacity to contribute to economic and social goals. These particular discourses have contributed to the increased interest in early childhood services by government and policy.

> In the field of early years, the technologies and processes include working with detailed and prescriptive curricula (or similar practice guidelines), programmes and similar procedures to regulate methods of working, and using observation and other methods to assess performance against developmental norms and other standardized outcome criteria. (Moss, 2006, p. 35)

These characterizations have inspired the creation of hundreds of thousands of early childhood programs across North America, many of these programs for the specified purposes of supporting maternal employment, improving the economy, enhancing child learning outcomes, and intervening with biological, economic, and social disadvantage (Scarr, 1998).

When applied to early childhood education, the image of educators' work as engineered technique implies that there exists one chief, scripted sequence of curriculum practices that produces desirable outcomes that can, and in many circumstance should, be generalized to all situations. This image also implies that in order to produce and maximize those desirable outcomes across programs, jurisdictions should pursue regulating them. This idea is associated with the social image that the field of early childhood education is not a sophisticated field to understand or navigate. Parallel to this image are two associated views. The first of these is the view that in order to work in this field all that is required is the learning of a number of specific techniques that will be applied over and over with little thought or need to critically examine or create anything original. The second of these is the view that in order for educators to implement curriculum practices that produce and maximize desirable outcomes in programs, their practices should be governed by regulations.

While detailed and prescriptive techniques in the form of kits and step-by-step curriculum ideas offer promises of developmental gains by children that are associated with raising the importance of early childhood education and the profile of educators, those concerned with the professional identity of educators have voiced their apprehensions regarding their presence in early childhood classrooms. According to those who are concerned with the professional identity of educators, such curriculum materials contribute to limiting the view of educators to mere technicians who implement predetermined technologies of others through regulated processes, rather than as educated professionals capable of contextual decision-making (Fenech & Sumsion, 2007; Osgood, 2006b).

The findings of a study carried out by Fenech and Sumsion (2007) examining how early childhood educators experience regulatory processes and accountabilities reveal that regulating curriculum practices is perceived by educators as constraining to their professional decision-making capabilities. Sixteen university-qualified early childhood educators, working in full day day-care in Australia, were individually interviewed about their experiences with regulatory accountabilities. Interview data were analyzed for content and emerging themes. Findings revealed that participants perceived prescriptive regulations to be a general constraint on their practices, independence, and time. Participants reported that the majority of regulations prevented them from supporting children's natural curiosity and extending learning. This was especially true when regulations were specific and prescriptive in cases where materials that had been detailed by the regulations as potentially dangerous were in question. In these situations, regulations, and those applying the regulations, did not consistently recognize educators as competent professionals with abilities to judge whether or not materials present a danger within the context of a situation and to problem-solve these situations independently (Fenech & Sumsion, 2007). It has also been suggested that the association of educator work with technique devalues care and emotional labour as cornerstones essential to the early childhood profession, and to the professional identities of those who work as educators (Osgood, 2006b). What is more, it presents educators as being incapable of problem solving, deep thinking, and co-constructing curriculum within the context of learning situations (Moss, 2006).

A third image of early childhood educators that is emerging in literature is that of the educator as researcher (Moss, 2006; Nimmo & Park, 2009). The educator as researcher is associated with discourses of knowledge co-construction through relationships with theories, children, families, and colleagues; critical examination and analysis of ideas; and reflection of practices. For the educator who views herself as researcher, research is not only an essential tool of practice, "it is a response to curiosity and doubt. It constructs new knowledge, it makes for critical thinking, is a part of citizenship and democracy" (Rinaldi & Moss, 2004, p. 3).

The image of the educator as researcher is associated with a view of the field of early childhood education as a valuable and complex structure of our society, and a view of the educator who works within that field as a critical thinker capable of considering multiple perspectives and complex professional decision-making. The association of the educator as researcher contributes to a social image of a person who is a knowledgeable and skilled professional capable of facilitating children's learning through innovative and unique curriculum practices that have not been handed down to her but have emerged through a collaborative process that relies on knowledge and capability.

50

With a view to transforming the traditional image of early childhood educators through participation in a research mentorship team initiative, Nimmo and Park (2009) carried out a two-year study that investigated the following three questions: (1) how does having opportunities to engage in research affect early childhood educators' identities?; (2) how do educators shift their paradigms regarding the nature of research through their research mentorship experience?; and (3) what are implications of the research mentorship team for reflective practice and the notion of educators as researchers in early childhood education? The goals of the research mentoring team initiative included the fostering of collaborative inquiry and the promoting of educator as researcher.

Study participants included seven female, degree prepared, early childhood educators working in a university laboratory child-care center in New England. The research mentoring teams met monthly to discuss topics that emerged from teachers' interests and questions. Two members of the faculty that were part of the research team facilitated the meetings. Data were collected through semi-structured interviews, participant observations, audio taping of meetings, and document analysis. The data were then analyzed for emerging themes with a particular interest in patterns of shifting views of educators' professional identity in relation to engagement in research practices (Nimmo & Park, 2009).

Findings of this study reveal a consistent thread of the following four themes: changing research paradigms, the existence of a professional community of practice, commitment to the collaborative process, and opportunities to engage in a deep dialogue and intellectual process. Participants reported significant shifts in their orientations to research. These shifts contributed to positive changes in perceptions of self as capable researchers by the end of the study, a view they reported as previously attributing to academics not to early childhood educators. The authors of the study suggest that the process of participating in action research is an empowering one for early childhood

51

educators that may contribute significantly to shifting professional identity into a more positive direction (Nimmo & Park, 2009).

Similar to the professional identity of nurses (Clifford, 1992; Crawford et al., 2008; Salvage, 2006), and elementary and secondary teachers (Beijaard et al., 2000; Volkmann & Anderson, 1998), the professional identity of early childhood educators cannot easily be separated from the images that the public has of the value of their work, the capabilities of the children with whom they work, or of society's view of their field as a profession. Public views of educators have been described as low-level babysitters and surrogate mothers (McGillivray, 2008; Nimmo & Park, 2009); the children with whom they work have been described as being more in need of caretaking and loving than educating (Moss, 2006); and their work has been assessed as mindless, custodial work and as techniques that can be easily reproduced and duplicated (Kagan & Cohen, 1997; Moss, 2006). The influence of public views on the self-image of educators is evidenced by a pan-Canadian study that revealed only 19.9% of the educators surveyed reported a perception that professionals in other fields respected their work, and only 8.2% reported a perception that the general public respected the work in which they were engaged (Doherty et al., 2000).

The identity that educators develop of themselves as professionals is inter-connected with the perceptions that society has of work in which they engage and the value society places on that work. These societal perceptions cannot easily be separated from the unique belief systems that educators develop over time about the ways in which they should carry out their work, value of that work and the capabilities of the children with whom they work. Collectively, these elements contribute to their daily curriculum practices.

Rationale for the Present Study

A review of the literature and research investigating early childhood practices indicate that constructivist-inspired practices are positively associated with children's

52

learning outcomes (Arnett, 1989; Maccoby & Lewis, 2003; Whitebrook et al., 1990). Consequently, a significant number of early childhood experts in North America promote the implementation of constructivist-inspired curriculum practices in early childhood programs (Bennett, 2005; Dahlberg et al., 2007; DeVries & Kohlberg, 1990; DeVries et al., 1991; Jones et al., 2001; Katz, 1999). However, a closer examination of the research and literature devoted to examining curriculum practices in early childhood programs reveals that constructivist-inspired curriculum practices are not consistently present in early childhood programs (Charlesworth et al., 1993; File & Gullo, 2002; Kontos & Dunn, 1993; McMullen & Alat, 2002; Phillipsen et al., 1997).

Collectively, these findings highlight the complicated nature of implementing curriculum practices in early childhood programs, and specifically highlight educators' beliefs (Cassidy & Lawrence, 2000; Wilcox-Herzog & Ward, 2004) and professional identity (Fenech & Sumsion, 2007; Kashin, 2009; Nimmo & Park, 2009) in association with the implementation of curriculum practices. These findings emphasize educators' unique beliefs as complicated constructs that are influenced by a number of factors including individual perceptions, professional knowledge and past experiences (Green, 1971; Kagan, 1992; McGillivray, 2008; Moss, 2006; Pajares, 1992; Richardson, 2003).

The recent focus on educators' professional identity draws attention to the associations among various social discourses, educators' views of themselves and their profession, their beliefs about curriculum, and subsequent practices (McGillvray, 2008; Kashin, 2009; Moss, 2006). Drawing on early childhood literature and research, it appears that early childhood educators are not consistently implementing practices endorsed by their profession and taught by their training colleges. A significant body of research suggests that educators' curriculum practices are vulnerable to the influence of educators' beliefs (Cassidy & Lawrence, 2000; Wilcox-Herzog & Ward, 2004) and of educators' professional identity (Fenech & Sumsion, 2007; Moss, 2006).

As previously identified, the investigation of professional identity in early childhood education is an emerging field of study and, while explored more extensively in other countries, has received limited attention in Canada (Kashin, 2009; Langford, 2008). Also, the studies that have contributed to our understanding of professional identity have not fully explored the relationship among beliefs about curriculum, professional identity, and curriculum practices (McGillvray, 2008; Moss, 2006; Osgood, 2006a). Thus, the proposed study will examine the inter-relationship among professional identity, curriculum beliefs, and curriculum practices of early childhood educators, and will contribute to the research and literature about this emerging, significant topic.

Chapter 3: Method

The following chapter outlines the method used to investigate the inter-relationships of early childhood educators' curriculum practices, curriculum beliefs, and professional identities. The section begins with the research questions that guide the study and is followed by the method selected to investigate those questions. Next, I provide information about the research location, including the rationale for its selection. In order to adequately explain the research setting, I offer a description of the child-care landscape in Ontario, including the child-care system and the child-care curriculum. I then outline the characteristics of the participants who were invited to participate in this study. Following this, I provide information about the procedure, the measurements that were used for data gathering, and how data were analyzed. Finally, I describe how credibility and trustworthiness of the data were ensured.

Research Questions

The main research question guiding this study is: What are the relationships among curriculum practices, beliefs about curriculum, and professional identities in qualified early childhood educators? This central research question gives rise to the following secondary questions to be investigated:

1) What are qualified early childhood educators' curriculum practices?
2) What are qualified early childhood educators' self-reported beliefs about curriculum?
3) How do qualified early childhood educators describe their professional identity?
4) What are the relations among educational and professional backgrounds of qualified early childhood educators and their self-reported beliefs about

curriculum, their practices of curriculum, and their descriptions of professional identity?

Selecting a Method

The main research question that guided this study examined the inter-relationships among curriculum practices, curriculum beliefs, and professional identities. In order to carry out this investigation, I employed a mixed method research design that combined qualitative and quantitative research. In describing the decision to use mixed method research design, Porcino and Verhoef (2010) stress that a mixed method design should be used purposefully to add value, not only to increase the volume of data in a study. My purpose for selecting a mixed method research design was that of complementarity. I based this decision on the type of constructs I was investigating, curriculum practices, beliefs about curriculum and professional identity, and my goal of examining how these constructs relate with one another.

The investigation of curriculum practices is most reliably carried out through a validated assessment tool that includes direct observation of practices to produce quantitative data. I utilized data gathered through direct observations of curriculum practices in order to produce a more accurate profile of participants' practices than might be achieved through self-reporting of those practices, which may be obscured by personal interpretations (Kane, 2000).

On the other hand, the examination of relationships among curriculum practices, curriculum beliefs, and professional identities involves an exploration of life experiences, understandings, and evolving beliefs of individuals that is context specific. It is an examination that is best carried out by using the qualitative research method of case study (Flyvbjerg, 2006; McMullen, et al., 2006). In the article *Five Misunderstandings about Case Study Research,* Flyvbjerg (2006) highlights that context-independent theory does not exist in the social sciences and identifies case study research as being well suited to producing context-specific knowledge about a human phenomenon. Case study research offers a "systematic exploration of multiple bounded systems through detailed, in-depth data collection involving multiple sources of information" (Creswell, 2007, p. 73).

A case study research method allowed me to examine how social structures, experiences, and processes interacted with each other in order to create a theory to explain emerging themes and happenings that evolved as a result of these interactions (Strauss & Corbin, 1998). This approach allowed me to achieve a deeper, more complete understanding of the relationships among the curriculum practices, curriculum beliefs, and professional identities of each individual participant.

Research Location

This research study was carried out in the province of Ontario. This geographical location was selected as a matter of convenience as it was within my ability to travel without placing extraordinary stress on budget and resources.

Child-Care Services in Ontario

As this study was carried out in Ontario, it is helpful to understand the child-care context of the province as it relates to services, curriculum and essential elements related to this study. Child-care services in Ontario include a combination of unlicensed and licensed sectors. The unlicensed sector is comprised of unlicensed family child-care and family resource centers. In unlicensed family child-care, up to five children under the age of 10 can be cared for in a private home ((*Day Nurseries Act*, R.S.O., 1990). This arrangement is similar to that of babysitting with no regulations governing the home and no government financial subsidies applied to paying for the care. Family resource centers offer a range of support services, such as drop-in programs, resource lending libraries, and playgroups to parents. In family

57

resource centers, children are not left in the care of the staff, and while there are no individual financial subsidies offered to parents to pay for this service, family resource centers do receive government grants to fund their services (Beach et al., 2009).

The licensed sector includes licensed center-based child-care and regulated or supervised private home day care. Licensed center-based child-care includes full day child-care centers, part day nursery schools, and before and after school programs. Both licensed center-based child-care and regulated private home day care adhere to regulations, and families that utilize these services are eligible for financial subsidies from the municipal or regional government (Beach et al., 2009).

In Ontario, licensed child-care centers are required to follow regulations set out by the *Day Nurseries Act* (R.S.O., 1990). These regulations include a number of specific requirements for each facility, including organization and management, allocation of space, choice of equipment and furnishings, health and nutrition, staff qualifications, staff numbers and ratio, group size, and curriculum.

Child-Care Curriculum in Ontario

In Ontario, the curriculum carried out in child-care has been described as a tapestry of various approaches, models, and philosophies (Friendly, Doherty, & Beach, 2006). While regulations governing the licensed child-care sector speak to curriculum (*Day Nurseries Act*, R.S.O., 1990) and the province has a conceptual curriculum framework, ELECT (Ministry of Children and Youth Services, 2006), the daily decisions surrounding the curriculum practices in the licensed child-care sector are largely left in the hands of the educators who work directly with children.

Regulations related to child-care curriculum are expressed in broad terms and the provincial curriculum framework ELECT includes a broad vision of beliefs, values and principles that is flexible enough to be interpreted at an individual program level. While the use of ELECT is voluntary for all early childhood programs in the province, the document has been widely distributed to early childhood settings within the province and has received considerable attention during the last six years (Beach, et al., 2009). The Ontario Ministry of Child and Youth Services engaged in a campaign to support the implementation of this framework in early childhood settings. This campaign has included making the document available to every licensed child-care center in the province, and the financial support of professional development activities to introduce the curriculum framework to practicing educators through workshops and conferences. In addition, post-secondary early childhood education programs have been encouraged to introduce the ELECT document to students during their course of study.

The curriculum framework provides broad guidelines intended to inform, not impose practice, and is purposefully designed to invite educators to "shift from prescribed, programmed curriculum to co-constructed curriculum based on negotiated beliefs, values, and principles related to early learning" (Whitty, 2009, p. 50). The absence of precise instructions as to how to translate this framework into curriculum practices contributes to a condition where educators' life experiences, understandings of curriculum, and evolving beliefs intersect and merge to influence daily curriculum practices. This condition created the circumstance that supported my investigation.

Research Setting

The research settings for this study included licensed child-care centers in Ontario. Licensed child-care centers were purposefully chosen for this study because they are the primary locations where qualified early childhood educators, the participants of this study, work (Beach et al., 2009).

Child-care centers for the study were recruited through letters that had been emailed to center supervisors. These letters contained information about the study and supervisors interested in having their center participate were invited to contact me by telephone or email by a specified date. As each supervisor interested in having their center participate contacted me, I followed up with each by sending the center consent forms approved by the University's Research Ethics Committee to sign and return. Once I received each signed center consent form, I proceeded to send educator participant information to each supervisor to distribute to center staff.

Participants

Practicing early childhood educators were invited to participate in this study. In agreement with case study research, practicing educators were purposefully selected as they were experiencing the phenomenon under study (Starks & Trinidad, 2011). Representative of the demographic population of early childhood educators in Ontario, the participating educators selected for this study held a post-secondary diploma or degree in Early Childhood Education from a recognized post-secondary educational institution and worked in licensed child-care centers with preschool aged children (Beach et al., 2009).

As precise guidelines associated with numbers of participants required for qualitative research were difficult to locate, determining the number of participants for the study was not obvious. Guidelines that were uncovered emphasized the importance of utilizing a flexible approach to sampling, and highlighted the importance of continuing to gather data until saturation occurred (Marshall, 1996; Strauss & Corbin, 1998). A study conducted to ascertain the number of interviews at which saturation occurs in qualitative research revealed that from a total of 60 in-depth interviews, no new themes emerged following the analysis of the first 12 interviews (Guest, Bunce, & Johnson, 2006). While literature specific to case study research does not clearly define the ideal number of cases required for a study in order to generate an explanation, it does suggest a number between four and 10 cases (Eisenhardt, 1989). The number of participants for this study was five. ―for this Study

60

Five individual educator participants were recruited from five separate licensed child-care centers that provided consent to participate in the study. An information letter, (included as Appendix A) about the study was sent to each center supervisor through email. Those supervisors who were interested in having their center participate contacted me and were sent letters (included as Appendix B) through email to be distributed to educators. Interested educators were invited to contact me by email or telephone by a specified date. Each participant who contacted me and met the qualifying characteristics was sent consent forms approved by the University's Research Ethics Committee through email to sign and return. As each participant returned a signed consent form, I contacted each one to negotiate and finalize dates and times for data gathering. As a professional courtesy, I also communicated these dates and times to each child-care center supervisor.

In the event that more than one educator who met the criteria for the study had volunteered to participate from a single child-care center, I planned to use a lottery system to make the final selection. Also, in the event that fewer than five participants who met the criteria volunteered for the study, I planned to expand the geographical location to include other nearby counties until five participants who met the required criteria had been recruited. As I was able to recruit five participants who met the criteria for the study from the planned geographical location, I was not required to implement these strategies.

Procedure

Data that were gathered for this study included observational assessments of curriculum practices; photographs of the physical classroom environment including various supporting curriculum documents, such as curriculum planning forms and child observation forms; professional background information of participants; participant self-reports of curriculum beliefs; and participant self-reports of professional identity. These multiple data collection methods provided a stronger substantiation of the constructs that were uncovered (Eisenhardt, 1989; McMullen, et al., 2006).

The instrumentation used to gather these data included an observational assessment of quality that captures classroom practices through the Classroom Assessment Scoring System (CLASS; Pianta, LaParo, & Hamre, 2008); photographs of classroom physical environment and curriculum documents; and a semi-structured interview process utilized by a previous study conducted to assess educator beliefs about curriculum (Howe, Jacobs, Vukelich, & Rechia, 2012) that I modified for the purpose of this study.

In each participant's classroom, the CLASS was administered first by an individual trained in the administration of the CLASS. Following this, the individual who administered the CLASS removed herself to a private location at the child care center site to score the results of the observation data where she produced a classroom profile of ratings associated with the curriculum practices of each participant. While this process occurred, I took photographs of each classroom's physical environment and of curriculum documents that were used by the participants in their programs. These photographs were taken after the children and the educators left the classroom to go outside. The last instrumentation used was the semi-structured interview that I conducted with each participant in a private location at the child-care center site. During this interview process, I utilized the classroom profile findings provided to me by the administrator of the CLASS and the photographs of the physical environment and curriculum documents to inspire conversation about the reasoning for curriculum practices with each participant. By following this procedure, I achieved a more complete understanding of why the participants implemented the curriculum practices observed, and how those practices related to the curriculum beliefs and professional identities each participant revealed during the interview process.

Measures

Classroom Assessment Scoring System (CLASS; Pianta, et al., 2008).
Developed as an extension to environment rating scales in order to reveal how educators initiate and respond to interactions with children, the CLASS focuses on classroom processes (LaParo, Pianta, & Stuhlman, 2004). Drawing from research on teacher-child relationships, classroom environments, and curriculum practices, the CLASS is an observational assessment of curriculum practices that emphasizes three domains of teacher-student interaction (Pianta et al., 2008). These three domains include emotional support, classroom organization, and instructional support.

Each of the three domains is divided into separate dimensions. The emotional support domain includes four dimensions (positive climate; negative climate; teacher sensitity; regard for student perspectives), the classroom organization domain includes three dimensions (behavior management; productivity; instructional learning formats), and the instructional support domain includes three dimensions (concept development; quality of feedback; language modeling). Each dimension is further divided into indicators that include observational characteristics that are used as the basis for the classroom observations. As an example, the domain of emotional support includes four dimensions, one of which is the dimension of positive climate. This positive climate dimension includes the indicators of relationships, positive affect, positive communication, and respect and each of these indicators is further operationalized into observable characteristics that tell a story of positive climate during the observation period. The indicator relationship is further defined as physical proximity, shared activities, peer assistance, matched affect, and social conversations. Appendix C summarizes the categories of the CLASS, as well as the observable characteristics under each indicator.

Four separate, consecutive 20-minute periods are observed and rated along each dimension. Each dimension is rated along a 1 to 7 point scale, with 1 to 2 indicating low levels, 3 to 5 medium levels, and 6 to 7 high levels. Following each observation cycle, an average rating for each dimension is calculated. These average dimension ratings are then utilized to determine an average rating for each corresponding domain (emotional support; classroom organization; instructional support). In determining domain ratings, the scores for negative climate are reversed.

The observational structure utilized by the CLASS has been validated in more than 3,000 classrooms (Hamre, Mashburn, Pianta, & Downer, 2006). The inter-rater reliability on the CLASS dimensions ranges from 78.8% for regard for student perspectives to 93.9% for negative climate and behavior management to 96.9% for productivity, with an overall inter-rater agreement of 87% within 1 point of each other (Pianta, et al., 2008).

Results of analyses examining criterion validity to assess relationships between CLASS and the Early Childhood Environment Rating Scale, Revised Edition (ECERS-R; Harmes, Clifford, & Cryer, 1998), a popular measure of quality assessment in early childhood classrooms, demonstrate a correlation of .63 ($p < .001$) between ECERS-R factor interactions and CLASS domain emotional support. The strength of this correlation has been attributed to the point that the ECERS-R interaction factor describes the extent to which classrooms promote teacher-child interactions, encourage communication and use of language, and engage in effective discipline; these are characteristics more closely associated with CLASS' focus on classroom interactions (Pianta, et al., 2008).

Two individuals other than me, trained in the administration of the CLASS observation assessment tool collected and scored the data for this study. These individuals were trained by an external instructor representing the official training organization of the CLASS instrument. The training took place over a two-day period and included an intense overview of the scoring process through the use of video segments of classroom events. These video segments were examined and described for the purpose of illustrating key behavioural indicators associated with specific scoring of the CLASS dimensions and domains. Following these two days of training, each

64

individual participated in 6 weeks of self-study and practice coding. Using the CLASS and the training video library accessed through a website of additional classroom events, each individual observed 20-minute video segments, scored the events observed, and reviewed the assigned scores against the master coding forms which were made available through the same website.

Following this self-study process, each individual participated in an on-line test. The test involved the observation of 5 random 20-minute video segments of classroom events and the scoring of those events using the CLASS observation instrument. The video segments used for the test were different than those segments that were used in the two-day training period and the self-study process. In order to become certified to administer the CLASS, each participant had to demonstrate reliability of scores within 1 point of the master code scores for each individual test video segment, plus for each dimension across all five video test segments. Each participant had to achieve a minimum reliability score of 80% across the ten dimensions (positive climate; negative climate; teacher sensitivity; regard for student perspective; behavior management; productivity; instructional learning formats; concept development; quality of feedback; language modeling) for each of the five individual test video segments. In addition, each participant had to achieve a score within 1 point of the master code scores for each dimension across all five test video segments for a minimum of two out of five video segments. Both individuals who administered the CLASS for this study achieved this level of reliability.

Neither of the individuals who collected and scored the CLASS data for this study had knowledge of any other data collected. The first individual watched and recorded, without interruption, classroom activity for a period of 20 minutes, over four separate, consecutive 20-minute cycles. Following each 20-minute period, each observation cycle was scored according to the dimensions of positive climate, negative climate, teacher sensitivity, regard for student perspectives, behavior management, productivity, instructional learning formats, concept development, quality of feedback, and language modeling that comprise the three domains (emotional support; classroom organization; and instructional support). Following the full observation cycle, a summary score sheet associated with these dimensions and domains was created.

Reliability of scoring was achieved by having the second individual administer the CLASS at the same time for 20% of the classroom data gathered (one classroom). The proportion of agreement between the two assessors was 70% for exact agreement and 97% for agreement within one point.

Photographs of classroom physical environments and curriculum documents. The arrangement of the physical classroom environment is an essential component of the curriculum practices of early childhood educators (Stacey, 2009). The manner in which the classroom is set up, and the equipment and the materials that are included in the classroom reflect the philosophical beliefs that educators hold about curriculum (Katz, 1999). Curriculum documents, such as daily routine, curriculum planning forms, and child observation forms, are familiar tools-of-the trade of early childhood education (Goffin, 2000). Not only do these resources assist educators in the implementation of daily curriculum practices, but the way in which they are designed and expressed reflects pedagogical beliefs and principles of curriculum.

In order to strengthen the reliability of information gathered through the CLASS observational tool and the interview process, I took photographs of the classroom physical environment and curriculum documents with the expressed permission of each participant. In doing this, I made sure that no photographs included images of children or distinguishing marks that might identify a center by name. Additionally, I invited each participant to provide me with blank copies of the curriculum documents that they were using in their program. During the subsequent interview process, I asked each participant to describe how and why each curriculum document was used in the program. I inquired about the process of how these documents were developed, and specifically about their involvement in that development.

This strategy is consistent with investigation procedures used in other research. In a study examining the relationship between pedagogical beliefs and classroom strategies, investigators collected course material distributed to students such as syllabi and test forms as significant data sources (Hativa, Barak, & Simhi, 2001). In a related study examining the relationship between self-reported beliefs and documentable practices of preschool educators, the researchers used surveys, observations of practices, and a collection of classroom documents (photographs; sketches of room arrangement; daily schedules; program descriptions; brochures; printed curriculum materials; and newsletters) to carry out their investigation (McMullen et al., 2006).

Educator Interview. The educator interview used for this study was a modification of one that had been successfully used in a previous study examining educator curriculum beliefs (Howe, et al, 2012). A copy of the educator interview is included in Appendix D. The interview format has been used successfully in previous studies to examine individuals' views of teaching (Dall'Alba, 1991; Howe et al, 2012; Johnston, 1996).

The educator interview followed a semi-structured format and lasted approximately one hour. The interview included three separate sections: a professional background section, a section that explained observed practices, and one that specifically focused on beliefs. I conducted the interview with each educator in a private location at the child-care center, and with permission, audio taped each interview. All audiotapes were transcribed.

The first section of the interview focused on professional background and included eight questions pertaining to highest credential obtained, years of experience in the field, prior employment, and type of professional development experienced. The second section of the interview focused on explanations of observed practices. This section was created to gain a deeper understanding of curriculum practices and was inspired by the assessment data obtained through the CLASS and by the photographs taken of classroom physical environment and curriculum documents. This section

67

proceeded as a conversation that referenced the assessment data collected through the previously recorded CLASS observations and the photographs that had been taken. The conversation proceeded according to the flow of the observed time frame of each program. I began by making reference to the previous data-gathering episode, stating, "As you remember, (name of individual) was here on _____ and observed you in your program. I would like to speak with you about some of those observations." During each interview, I made reference to observations recorded during the assessment and invited each participant to expand on what had occurred and to describe what led them to the curriculum practices previously observed, recorded, and scored. For example, I referred to an observation gathered through the CLASS and asked, "Can you tell me more about that incident?" The responses from each participant gave rise to conversations guided by questions, such as these: "How did you come to decide to do that?" "Tell me about your intentions in introducing or participating in that experience", "Where did you learn to do that?," "How do parents respond when that occurs in the classroom?," and "Why do you think they respond in that way?" This approach allowed me to engage in more authentic and meaningful conversations with each participant, and to confirm data that were gathered through the CLASS.

The third section of the interview deepened the focus on beliefs about curriculum practices and professional identity. This section was designed to elicit additional thoughts about the association between curriculum and professional identity. During this portion of the interview, I asked open-ended questions, such as "How would you describe the curriculum in your program?" and "How would you describe qualities required to be an effective educator?" In addition to these questions, I also included 11 incomplete statements that I asked each participant to complete. Examples of these statements include: "The reason I became an early childhood educator is …," and "The parents of the children in my program view my work as ..."

Through guided conversation, I posed open-ended questions to elicit educators' thoughts and beliefs about curriculum and professional identity, and to describe the

68

reasoning behind their curriculum practices. Questions were asked in a manner to avoid offering clues that might have contributed to participants' providing professionally desirable answers, or focusing on theoretical suppositions that might not have reflected actual experiences (Kane, 2000). I avoided asking participants directly to describe their professional identity, or to specifically categorize their beliefs and practices as being inspired by either a constructivist or an instructivist curriculum framework.

Interviews with each participant were conducted in a private location at the child-care center work site. Each interview lasted about one hour. Prior to being used for this study, the educator interview questions and format were piloted with a qualified early childhood educator who worked in a licensed child-care lab school facility. The results of the pilot lead to minor changes to the interview questions and contributed to a smoother flow of the actual interview process and a more natural conversation with the educators.

Analysis of Findings

Multiple data sources have contributed to the findings of this research study. These findings were documented through three distinct approaches. The first approach included narrative descriptions of each participant's professional background including demographic information, professional qualifications, and professional development experiences; narrative descriptions of each participant's expansions and explanations of curriculum practices; and narrative descriptions of each participant's beliefs about curriculum and professional identity. The second approach included photographs of the classroom physical room arrangements and curriculum documents associated with each participant. The third approach included graphs that illustrate the average ratings each participant achieved through the CLASS observation tool.

These findings have been examined for recurring themes across all cases. First, I employed a within-case analysis to analyze the findings uncovered through the CLASS observation tool, the educator interviews, and the photographs taken of classroom physical environments and curriculum documents for each individual case. Second, I revisited and re-examined the findings uncovered through educator interviews, classroom photographs, curriculum documents, and CLASS ratings for the purpose of identifying emerging themes across all cases. I present a detailed description of the themes that emerged across all cases according to the following dimensions: professional background (professional qualifications; professional development experiences), curriculum practices (classroom physical environment and curriculum documents; graph of CLASS ratings; expansions of educator practices), descriptions of curriculum beliefs, and descriptions of professional identity. I then offer an interpretation of the meaning of these data.

Narrative Analysis

In addition to the data collected through the observation assessment CLASS, these case studies represent the stories of these educators' curriculum practices, beliefs about curriculum, and professional identities as told to me. Reporting the findings from these five cases as objective would be neither an accurate nor truthful representation, as they intertwine with my own personal narrative of early childhood learning and experience. I have been in the field of early childhood education for over 27 years and have worked as an educator, a professor of early childhood education, a consultant of curriculum practices, and an administrator in the provincial government responsible for child-care funding and regulations. During my years in this field I have encountered thousands of early childhood education students and practicing educators and have worked with them as they struggled to translate curriculum theory into practice. My specific focus of examining how beliefs about curriculum shape curriculum practices and eventually intertwine with professional identity has been profoundly influenced by my experiences in the field of early childhood education and by the number of educators I have been privileged to work with.

This personal narrative is a part of me as researcher that I acknowledge and recognize as influencing and contributing to my analysis of these findings. "There is no formula or recipe for the best way to analyze the stories we elicit and collect" (Coffey & Atkinson, 1996, p. 80). While I have attempted to document the stories that have been told to me in a way to allow the voices of the participants to be central, I acknowledge that my own voice has undoubtedly been inserted into this process and has contributed to the shaping of these cases and the eventual interpretations they have inspired.

Ensuring Credibility and Trustworthiness

In carrying out this investigation, I took steps to ensure the methodological rigor of the study associated with the transferability and dependability of results (Lincoln & Guba, 2000). First, I selected educators with characteristics similar to those of the early childhood workforce in Ontario to participate in this study. This practice makes the results of this study more credible. Second, I acquired the co-operation of two individuals who were trained in the administration and scoring of the CLASS, to gather the classroom observation assessment data. To preserve the integrity of the study, neither of these individuals was aware of any other data gathered in this study. The first individual administered and scored the CLASS in all participating classrooms, and the second individual conducted a reliability check for 20% of the classroom data gathered. Next, I utilized the observations that were gathered as a component of administering the CLASS as the springboard for my conversations with participants about their beliefs about curriculum and professional identity. This process allowed for a form of member-checking as participants had an opportunity to clarify the recorded observations. In addition, this process allowed for a more authentic conversation about curriculum beliefs as actual practices that had just been observed were discussed. Finally, findings from classroom observations, educator interviews, and curriculum documents were triangulated to examine the relationships among curriculum practices, curriculum beliefs, and professional identities.

Chapter 4: Findings

The following chapter presents the findings of this study and the analysis of those findings. First, I report the findings of each individual case study according to the following sequence: professional background; curriculum practices; and descriptions of educator beliefs. Then, I present an analysis of those findings.

Next, I present a description of the recurring themes across all cases and provide an analysis of those themes. I present this information according to the following sequence: emerging themes related to professional background of participants (professional qualifications; professional development), emerging themes related to curriculum practices (classroom physical environment and curriculum documents; a summary of mean scores of CLASS ratings for three domains; a summary of mean scores of CLASS ratings for individual dimensions within each domain; expansions of educator practices), emerging themes related to descriptions of educators' beliefs about curriculum, and emerging themes related to descriptions of educators' professional identity.

Descriptions of Each Case Study

The following section presents the findings associated with professional background, curriculum practices, and educator beliefs of each case study. The first section, professional background, is presented through narrative descriptions of each participant's educational background, employment history, and professional development experiences. The second section, curriculum practices, is presented in three segments: classroom physical environment and curriculum documents, CLASS ratings of educator curriculum practices, and expansions of educator practices. These segments are illustrated through narrative descriptions, photographs, and charts of CLASS ratings of the three domains (emotional supports; classroom organization supports; instructional supports). The third section, descriptions of educator beliefs, is presented through narrative descriptions.

Case Study Narratives

Luba

Professional background

Luba is a graduate of a two-year Early Childhood Education diploma program. Her diploma is the required qualification for working in a licensed child-care facility in the province she works. Since she graduated, Luba has worked as an early childhood educator in the same licensed child-care center. She has worked with children of various ages, from toddlers to school age children. At the time of this study, Luba was working in the preschool program with children between the ages of three to five years. In this program, Luba was one of three teachers working with 24 children.

While working as an early childhood educator, Luba had engaged in a number of professional development activities. During the last year, she attended four separate professional development workshops, ranging from 1.5 to 2.5 hours in length. Her decision to attend these workshops was motivated by an interest in continued learning. Luba's qualification as an early childhood educator does not require her to participate in professional development, and while her workplace encourages and supports professional development, it is not required as a condition of employment. All four workshops were delivered in the evenings after working hours at an off-site location, a local professional resource center.

Luba described the major subject matter of all four workshops as "curriculum related." She decided to attend these workshops on her own initiative and stated, "I enjoy learning new curriculum ideas." As is policy in the child-care center where Luba works, she paid half of the fee for each of the workshops that she attended and her employer paid the other half of the fee.

Curriculum practices

Classroom physical environment and curriculum documents. The classroom environment in Luba's program was spacious and bright. The hallway leading into the classroom was decorated with two bulletin boards that were at adult height. The first bulletin board contained a copy of the monthly calendar, the daily schedule for the program, a listing of the activities planned for that week, a half-filled curriculum web form (see Figure 1.1), and a curriculum brainstorming form (see Figure 1.2). The monthly calendar highlighted special events taking place that month. These included children's birthdays, days the center was to be closed, and days referred to as Show and Share Days, when children would bring special items from home to share and discuss with their classmates. Special focal points emphasized through the curriculum, such as letters of the week that teachers were concentrating on with the children were also included in this calendar.

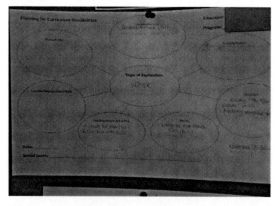

Figure 1.1. Half-filled curriculum web form

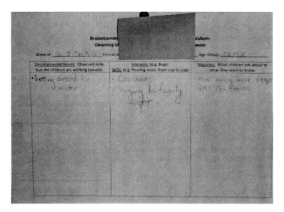

Figure 1.2. Curriculum brainstorming form

The second bulletin board contained a series of pictures documenting the children's interest in music and dancing. These pictures were posted at adult height and were accompanied by written anecdotes of how the children's interest in this topic arose, and how it translated into the children's play that evolved over the weeks.

Across from the bulletin boards was a half wall that opened into the classroom space. On the ledge of this wall was a notebook that educators used to record significant information that parents provided when they dropped off their children. The classroom space was divided into play centers that were located around the periphery of room. The play centers (art, sand, water, blocks, dress-up, computers, and books) were well organized and the materials within each one were clearly labeled through the use of pictures. These play centers provided a generous array of materials that were easily accessible to children (see Figure 1.3). The middle of the classroom contained three tables with chairs around them. This space was used for meals and teacher-planned activities.] - teacher-lead ﹒

Figure 1.3. Well organized play center with easily accessible material

Posted on another wall in the classroom, at adult height, was a curriculum web. The focus of the web was winter and it was filled with activity ideas associated with winter.

CLASS ratings of educator practices.

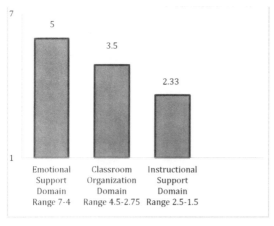

Figure 1.4. Mean scores for Emotional Support Domain, Classroom Organization Domain, and Instructional Support Domain

The CLASS ratings of Luba's curriculum practices (see Figure 1.4) indicated a middle level rating for the Emotional Support Domain (5) and for the Classroom Organization Support Domain (3.5), and a low level rating for the Instructional Support Domain (2.33). These ratings were based on mean scores assigned to each of the 10 dimensions that comprised the three domains with the highest score assigned to a inverted score for the dimension of negative climate (7) and the lowest score assigned to the dimension of concept development (1.5).

Within the domain of Emotional Support, the range of ratings associated with the four individual dimensions varied from an inverted score of 7 (negative climate) to a score of 4 (teacher sensitivity). Within the domain of Classroom Organization Support, the range of ratings associated with three individual dimensions varied from a score of 4.5 (productivity) to 2.75 (behavior management). Within the domain of Instructional Support, the range of ratings associated with the three individual dimensions varied from a score of 3 (language modeling) to a score of 1.5 (concept development).

Expansions of educator practices. Luba provided a warm and welcoming atmosphere for the children. She greeted each child by name as they entered the classroom, often bending down to their level and gently touching their arm or shoulder. She moved around the classroom and spoke with children as they played in various play centers. Her tone of voice was pleasant and non-threatening as she communicated with them.

As she moved around the classroom during free-play time, Luba did not linger in any one area for very long. She dropped in on play activities that were occurring and offered comments, such as, "That row of blocks is getting long," or "I guess we'll have to get a new pillow." She asked questions such as, "How many blocks do you have?", and when children asked her a question about the program or about their play, Luba provided short and accurate answers.

During one of the observation periods, Luba carried out a circle time activity with a focus on one specific letter. This focus was associated with a prepackaged literacy program that the child-care center was using at the time. As part of this activity, Luba used a CD that offered a number of words that began with the same letter and the children were directed to repeat the words and to mimic particular actions. When the children lost interest in the activity, Luba gently redirected their attention to focus on the voice from the CD and the task at hand related to the letter.

Descriptions of educator beliefs

In describing her beliefs about curriculum, Luba emphasized the importance of observing children. She indicated that observing children and documenting those observations were important to her in deciding what type of activities to plan for, because it allowed her "to know their [the children's] interests and things they are working towards or need help with." She highlighted the importance of having a flexible approach to curriculum that was not bound by specific schedules. Luba revealed that play was an important part of curriculum and added that she believes children learn many concepts through play.

Luba categorized the curriculum approach that she followed as being emergent. To her, it meant following the children's interests. She states, "Because it's Halloween does not mean we have to talk about Halloween. It's seeing what the kids are interested in and just going with their interest." Our conversation drifted into the use of curriculum webs as a strategy for illustrating how curriculum evolves within an emergent curriculum approach. In describing her thoughts about curriculum webs, Luba expressed the importance of involving the children in generating activity ideas, and emphasized their capabilities by stating, "You would be amazed at how much information they have."

In further conversation about the specific curriculum web posted on the wall in the classroom and how it came to be, Luba informed me that the web was created by one of her coworkers. As our conversation unfolded, Luba confirmed that none of the activities that took place on the day of my visit was related to the activities posted on the curriculum web.

In discussing beliefs about curriculum, on several occasions Luba indicated reasoning behind her curriculum decisions is associated with others. The final decision to follow the prepackaged literacy curriculum was linked with an elementary teacher who had worked in that classroom years before, credit for the curriculum web and the design of the curriculum form posted on the program bulletin board were connected to another educator. Luba's thoughts about these curriculum elements seemed to be neutral. While she indicated that she did not mind the form, she also maintained that the form did not provide her with the ability to capture the children's interests beyond the focus of the week. Even though she declared that the curriculum web was beneficial, she did not refer to any activities or ideas recorded on the web. Finally, her description of the prepackaged language program she was using revealed that she thought it was good because an elementary school teacher introduced it to the program.

Luba described effective educators as, "loving and caring, understanding towards all children's needs, and flexible." This description was central to her description of her day-to-day work with young children and to her explanation of the importance of that work. Luba described educators as surrogate parents who are stand-ins while the parents are working. She stated, "They've entrusted us with their kids," and "They [the children] miss their moms and dads, and we have to understand their feelings." This impression of the educator as surrogate parent was also present as Luba described the most difficult aspects of her work as an educator. Her explanation blurred the lines between the role of educator and the role of parent as she explained that going home to her own family could be draining after a full day of working as an educator because, "then you go home and basically start again."

In considering how others view her work with children, Luba proclaimed that they should think she is exceptional because she is patient. In recalling reasons why she became an educator, Luba emphasized her love for children and how her family members had often commented on this. She also revealed that because others pointed out her qualities of being caring and understanding, she had considered studying social work, and is confident that if she were not an educator, she would have become a social worker.

Luba's descriptions about her curriculum decisions were brief and revealed a focus on others as the decision makers. The curriculum form that she used in the program and the prepackaged literacy program that was the main source of her circle time activity were both curriculum elements that she described as having been introduced into the program by others. Even though Luba described the planning form as being incomplete in allowing her to fully capture children's play, she continued to use it in its current form. Although she acknowledged that the children struggled at times with the activities associated with the prepackaged literacy program, she continued to use it without modification adding that the educators who introduced it were teachers and that parents liked it "because we are doing things so their children can learn." The focus on others was extended as Luba explained that coworkers played a key role in influencing the ways in which she carried out curriculum.

Nada

Professional background

Nada holds a diploma in Early Childhood Education that qualifies her to work in a licensed child-care center in Ontario. Throughout her career, Nada has worked with various age groups (infants, toddlers, and school aged children) and she has worked both part-time and full-time. During all this time she has worked for only one organization and reported feeling fortunate to be with this organization.

While working as an educator, Nada reported that she participated in numerous professional development activities, and estimated that she probably participated in three to four different professional development events each year. Nada was proud to add that her workplace encouraged professional development and financially supported staff members who engaged in ongoing education by paying the fees associated with professional development events. She revealed that the organization's commitment to professional growth and development was one of the reasons she has stayed with them throughout her career.

During the last year, Nada attended four separate professional development workshops each ranging from two to three hours in length. The decision to attend two of the four workshops was mandated by her workplace. The topics for these two workshops included (1) an introduction to emergent curriculum and the ELECT document and (2) using observation to capture children's interests for documentation. Nada reported that the child-care center was motivated to make changes to their curriculum approach as a result of the provincial document ELECT and its endorsement of an emergent curriculum approach. A consultant, external to the organization, was hired by child-care center administration to deliver both of these workshops. Staff members were paid overtime to attend both workshops, which took place at the child-care center after work hours. Nada's assessment of these workshops was positive as she declared support for this approach to curriculum and indicated that the consultant offered excellent strategies for implementing emergent curriculum practices that were immediately useful to her practices. She specifically highlighted the forms that were shared for recording observations of children's interests.

Nada's decision to attend the other two workshops was due to the topics of those workshops. They interested her. Both of these workshops were delivered in the evenings, off-site. Nada's workplace paid full tuition for both workshops and she was able to take time off from work responsibilities because she attended these workshops.

The time off that was given to her equated the number of hours that she participated in the workshops.

Curriculum practices

Classroom physical environment and curriculum documents. The classroom environment in Nada's program was spacious and inviting. There was a bright and cheery atmosphere enhanced by streams of light emanating from six large windows. One wall of the classroom included samples of children's artwork, while two other walls displayed documentations of children's work clustered around the alphabet.

A large poster with the phrase Area of Development was mounted in a frame that hung on the wall just outside the classroom door. The poster included information about the area of development that was the focus of classroom activities and the skills associated with that area of development. Inside the classroom hung another poster that included a planning web that described the classroom curriculum experiences for that week.

The classroom space was divided into play centers that were located around the periphery of the room, allowing for smooth traffic flow as children moved from one play center to another. The play centers included an art area, sand table, water table, a blocks area, a dress-up area, and a library area. Each play center included sufficient space for the children to play in without unintentionally disturbing each other. Each play center was generously equipped, and the materials within each were well organized and easily accessible to the children (see Figure 2.1).

Figure 2.1. Well organized play center with easily accessible materials

The materials within each play center were clearly labeled through the use of pictures and drawings. Two tables were located in the middle of the room, which were used for children to work on during free-play time, for teacher-planned small group activities, and for meal times. In the corner of the classroom was a large poster of the letter S that has been decorated. The poster was surrounded by a number of posted documentation forms. The format of each documentation form was identical and included a picture of children, recorded observations of children decorating the letter and skills that were learned through the experience. These documentation forms were posted at adult height.

CLASS ratings of educator practices.

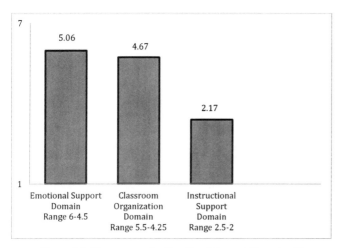

Figure 2.2. Mean scores for Emotional Support Domain, Classroom Organization Domain, and Instructional Support Domain

The CLASS ratings of Nada's curriculum practices (see Figure 2.2) indicated a middle level rating for the Emotional Support Domain (5.06) and for the Classroom Organization Support Domain (4.67), and a low level rating for the Instructional Support Domain (2.17). These ratings were based on mean scores assigned to each of the 10 dimensions that comprised the three domains with the highest mean score assigned to the dimension of positive climate (6) and the lowest mean score assigned to the dimensions of concept development and quality of feedback (2).

Within the domain of Emotional Support, the range of ratings associated with the four individual dimensions varied from a score of 6 (positive climate) to a score of 4.5 (regard for student perspectives). Within the domain of Classroom Organization Support, the range of ratings associated with three individual dimensions varied from a score of 5.5 (productivity) to 4.25 (behavior management). Within the domain of Instructional Support, the range of ratings associated with the three individual dimensions varied from a score of 2.5 (language modeling) to a score of 2 (concept development; quality of feedback).

Expansions of educator practices. Nada provided a warm and encouraging atmosphere for the children. When speaking with children, she bent down to their level and spoke to them in a calm and respectful tone. She often used children's names in conversation and smiled as she interacted with them. Nada moved around the classroom during free-play time initiating contact with children in various play areas. The contact Nada initiated was often in the form of questions, such as, "What letter is this?", "What color is this?", or "Can you find the blue block?" The children were generally able to answer these questions, and when they did, Nada left the area they were in and moved on to others.

Nada carried out an activity with a group of children during free-play focusing on a particular letter. She invited children to participate and involved them in gathering the materials they would need to carry out the activity. Nada and the children gathered on the carpet around a large letter that Nada constructed with yellow tape. She invited the children to trace the letter with their fingers and offered paper, markers and encouragement as the children copied the letter. Nada offered smiles and praise when the children completed their work and was especially attentive to those who seemed to struggle. She guided those children and gently reminded them that they could do it because she remembered seeing them copy another letter the day before.

Descriptions of educator beliefs

In describing her beliefs about curriculum, Nada highlighted play as an important aspect of children's learning. She maintained that learning happens naturally as children engage in play activities and explained that educators must learn how to recognize learning in children's play. She elaborated that learning is all around and that children are naturally drawn to learning through their play and that they are very capable learners.

Nada labeled the curriculum approach that she follows as being emergent. She explained that to her being emergent means observing what children are interested in, and then planning activities around those interests. In describing her thoughts about curriculum, Nada revealed that she had always approached curriculum in this same way throughout her career as an educator. She declared a firm commitment to play as the central principle of a quality curriculum and a major contributor to guiding children's learning.

As our conversation evolved, Nada described her curriculum planning process. She demonstrated great delight in walking me through the planning web that was posted on the wall of her classroom and emphasized that children's interests are the starting point for this process. Nada informed me that this curriculum web was introduced to the child-care center by an external consultant who conducted a workshop with all the staff members. She emphasized that the consultant was very good in that she provided them with all of the forms they use for their curriculum and told them exactly what to do. Nada expressed an appreciation for this clarity and consistency, and added that the forms are easy to use and "just have to be filled in."

In describing this process in greater detail, Nada explained that she and her colleagues use a specific form to capture their brainstorming and then translate that information to their planning form that focuses on development and observed interests of children in the program. She described in detail how each section of the planning web was associated with a specific skill area; however, as our dialogue progressed, Nada was not able to recall specific observations related to the activities and ideas recorded on the current planning web hanging in the classroom.

In response to describing what was currently happening in the program, Nada explained that they had been focusing on helping children learn letters and the alphabet through playful activities, such as tracing the letter activity. She revealed that learning these skills was important to children because they would be going to school soon and that parents get excited when their children can write.

Nada defined effective educators as "qualified teachers who know how to help children learn specific skills," and described her reason for becoming an early childhood educator as wanting "to help children learn." Learning skills was a theme that dominated Nada's work with children and her description of that work.

As our conversation unfolded, Nada revealed her belief that the parents of the children in her current program probably viewed her work to be important, but that she doubted this view was shared among the general public. She stated that she was most frustrated when people referred to her as babysitter. As our interview came to a close, Nada disclosed that if she had not become an early childhood educator, she would be "a teacher because she loves to help children learn."

Milena

Professional background

Milena was one of two educators in a preschool program with 16 children between the ages of three to five years. She had worked in the same licensed child-care center in which she began her work experience as an unqualified educator in 2005. Milena obtained her diploma in Early Childhood Education in 2009 after she completed a three-year Early Childhood Apprenticeship program through an Ontario college. The diploma provided her with the required credential to work as a qualified educator in a licensed child-care center. In addition to her diploma in Early Childhood Education, Milena has an unrelated degree.

During the last year, Milena had attended three professional development workshops ranging from two to three hours in length. The workshop topics included how to deal with behavior problems in your classroom, science activities with children, and how to create documentation panels. Her decision to participate in these workshops was motivated by an interest to learn new ideas related to her profession.

Her choice to attend these specific workshops was related to her program. She revealed that a significant number of behavior problems occurring with children in her classroom motivated her to sign up for the workshop dealing with behavior problems. She also revealed that the workshop was disappointing in that the information covered did not offer her any new strategies to try in her classroom. She did, however, indicate that the curriculum workshop on documentation was very informative and useful, and that the information presented inspired her to try documenting children's experiences.

The three workshops that Milena attended were delivered in the evenings, after working hours, at an off-site location. Milena's employer did not require her to participate in professional development as a condition of employment, but did support her by fully paying for all three of the workshops.

Curriculum practices

Classroom physical environment and curriculum documents. Milena's program took place in two adjoining classrooms located in a large building. A long corridor led into the first classroom that included a posted copy of the daily schedule for the preschool program, the monthly calendar, and the weekly curriculum form. The monthly calendar provided information about children's birthdays occurring that month, days the center would be closed, and any special events that would take place during that month. The weekly curriculum form contained information about the activities that had been planned by the educators for that week. The form included how curriculum categories, such as music/movement, language, and literacy would be covered throughout the week and listed names of activities.

This first room included the majority of the play areas and play materials (creative area, house area, sand table, block area) while the second classroom was the room where circle time took place, and included an adult-sized chair located in the corner and a shelf filled with children's books. The shelves in each play area were well organized and equipped with sufficient materials for children to use that they could easily access (see Figure 3.1). The classroom walls in both rooms were decorated with a combination of commercially created posters and child-constructed creations. The commercially created posters were scattered throughout the classroom and highlighted concepts, such as weather, numbers, color charts, and calendar. The child-constructed creations were grouped together according to the focus of the activity and posted on various walls throughout the classroom (see Figure 3.2).

Figure 3.1. Sufficient materials easily accessible by children

Figure 3.2 Classroom decorations

Posted on the back of one classroom shelf was a documentation panel. This documentation panel included pictures of children participating in a classroom experience and language written by educators that described observations of children's reactions to the experience. This panel was posted at the children's eye level.

CLASS ratings of educator practices.

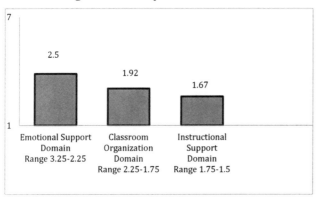

Figure 3.3. Mean scores for Emotional Support Domain, Classroom Organization Domain, and Instructional Support Domain

The CLASS ratings of Milena's curriculum practices (see Figure 3.3) indicated a low level rating for the Emotional Support Domain (2.5), the Classroom Organization Support Domain (1.92), and the Instructional Support Domain (1.67). These ratings were based on mean scores assigned to each of the 10 dimensions that comprised the three domains with the highest score assigned to the dimension of positive climate (3.25) and the lowest score assigned to the dimension of quality of feedback (1.5).

Within the domain of Emotional Support, the range of ratings associated with the four individual dimensions varied from a score of 3.25 (positive climate) to a score of 2.25 (teacher sensitivity; regard for student perspectives), and inverted score of 2.25 (negative climate). Within the domain of Classroom Organization Support, the range of ratings associated with three individual dimensions varied from a score of 2.25 (instructional learning formats) to 1.75 (behavior management; productivity). And, within the domain of Instructional Support, the range of ratings associated with the three individual dimensions varied from a score of 1.75 (concept development; language modeling) to a score of 1.5 (quality of feedback).

Expansions of educator practices. As children were playing, Milena moved around the classroom and paused in various play areas to remind children about classroom rules. Upon noticing children splashing water at the water table, she said, "You need to be careful, no spilling water," and upon observing one child hit another she stated, "Stop hitting and read your book."

As Milena moved around the classroom during free-play time, she paused in various play centers to interact with children. When a child held some pretend flowers to her face she smiled and uttered, "Oh, beautiful flowers, what colour are they?" and when the child responded, she praised him and moved to another part of the classroom.

During the observed period of snack time, the children turned their attention from snack to a visiting parent with a baby. They physically moved from the snack area to where the parent and the baby were sitting and began hugging and touching the baby, and cooing to the baby. Milena smiled and reminded them to come back and finish eating. The children returned to the snack table and their conversation about snack resumed.

Descriptions of curriculum beliefs

In describing her beliefs about curriculum, Milena highlighted the important role of curriculum in providing children with skills they will need for life. She expanded on this point and identified the specific skills of using scissors, respecting their friends, and socializing well with others as important life skills. Milena identified play as an important aspect of curriculum and stated, "Play is awesome, a very good opportunity for children."

Milena's approach to supporting children in socializing well with others was revealed as she described a conflict situation that occurred earlier that day when one child insisted on being the leader in the line-up to go to the bathroom. In describing this situation, Milena stated that she did not like the idea of having a leader, and when one child pushed another in order to be first in line, she told the children that they would not have a leader.

As our conversation about supporting children's socializing skills evolved, Milena revealed an external consultant who visited the program advised her to use a particular system to help children work well together. This system involved determining the number of children who could play in one area without interfering with one another and communicating that number to the children through the use of outlines of children or through the placement of the requisite number of chairs in that area. Milena reported that she used this system as a way to teach children to play well together.

In describing her approach to curriculum, Milena disclosed two opposing views. She referenced the ELECT document and described that children's interests are an important source for her curriculum practices. She explained that she had set up a teddy bear picnic in the dramatic play area as a result of children's conversations about their teddy bears. She also described a doubt about children's ability to provide her with sufficient material to make curriculum decisions and explained that children sometimes don't express enough information so she often referred to a list of themes. Milena reported that having the themes is helpful to educators as it clarifies what the curriculum focus is to be.

As we continued our conversation and walked around the classroom, Milena pointed out the children's art creations of reindeer that were posted on one of the walls. In describing how they came to be made, she revealed that she found the idea in a craft book and decided to carry out the activity because it was Christmas time and she thought the children would like it. In explaining how she carried out the activity, Milena described that she followed the instructions provided by the craft book in that she traced the children's footprints, cut out the tracings, and told the children that these would be the faces for the reindeer. The children then painted their hands to make hand print antlers. They knew to do this because Milena gave them instructions stating, "We're going to paint our hands and then you're going to print it to make the reindeer antlers." Milena indicated that her goal in providing this activity was to offer the children a sensory experience.

Milena reported that her curriculum decisions were also motivated by a desire to offer a program that makes children happy and is fun for them. She explained that it is important to her that children in her program are happy and enjoy their experiences. She described her belief that if children are happy they will learn more. In making this point, Milena referenced the special occasion days such as Pajama Day that she had inserted into the monthly calendar. Milena reported that she included these days and events to add fun to the program. Milena described effective educators as loving and patient individuals whose most important task was to make sure that the day runs smoothly and that children in their care were happy.

In describing her thoughts of how others viewed her work with children, Milena stated that people who were unfamiliar with the field of early childhood education perceived her work as babysitting. She added that she did not like that description. Milena attributed their opinion to not believing that children were important and that they could learn things in child-care centers. As our conversation turned to how the parents of the children in her program viewed her work, Milena took delight in recalling a story of a child who sat her parents in front of her at home and pretended to carry out a circle just like she does. She emphasized how pleased she was when that parent shared the story with her because it demonstrated to the parent how she teaches children important skills.

Nena

Professional background

Nena has worked as a full-time educator for 19 years. She obtained the required qualification (i.e., a diploma in Early Childhood Education) to work in a licensed child-care center from an Ontario college. During her career as a qualified educator, Nena had worked in three different child-care centers. She had always worked with children between the ages of three to five years, and had always worked full-time.

At the time of this study, Nena worked in the preschool program with children between the ages of three to five years, and was one of three full-time educators in that program. She had worked in her current position for seven years.

While working as an educator, Nena indicated that she had engaged in numerous professional development activities and declared that she usually attends three to four workshops every year. Nena's employer did not require her to participate in professional development as a condition of employment. She reported that she attends workshops because she enjoys learning new information and networking with new people at workshops.

During the past year, Nena attended three workshops. These workshops were delivered in the evenings, after working hours, at an off-site location. Her workplace paid half of the fee to attend the workshops and she paid the other half.

Nena reported that all of the workshops were very interesting and informative with the third workshop on emergent curriculum as the most informative. She emphasized that in addition to being informative, the workshop offered a collective opportunity for all staff members to discuss the value of implementing the emergent approach together and highlighted the value of the workshop in providing her with strategies to create curriculum webs. She also emphasized the documentation forms that were introduced through the workshop, adding that they were so easy to use; all she would have to do was to fill them out.

Curriculum practices

Classroom physical environment and curriculum documents. Hanging on the door leading into Nena's classroom was a large sign that focused parents' attention to the door. Under this sign, there were sheets of paper that included examples of children's experiences in the program. Each experience was illustrated through an identical documentation form that included a picture of a significant event, a written learning story of the event, and a listing of primary skills that had been demonstrated by children participating in the event.

Large windows that contributed to the bright and spacious feeling of the room dominated the classroom environment in Nena's program. Upon entering the classroom, a large bulletin board across the room catches the eye. This bulletin board, located at adult height, contained a copy of the preschool daily schedule and a copy of a large form, entitled planning web (see Figure 4.1). Additional forms that included illustrations of learning stories surrounded the planning web.

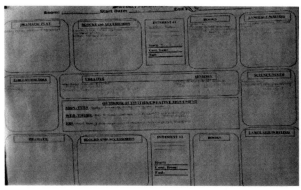

Figure 4.1 Planning web

The classroom space was divided into play centers around the room that included an art area, block area, dress-up area, sand and water area, and a quiet and library area. The play centers provided ample space for children to move about without interfering with each other's play, and were well equipped with materials that were easily accessible to children. The materials in each play center were organized and labeled with pictures and drawings. In the middle of the classroom there were three tables that were used by children during free-play and by educators and children during teacher-planned activities and meal times.

CLASS ratings of educator practices.

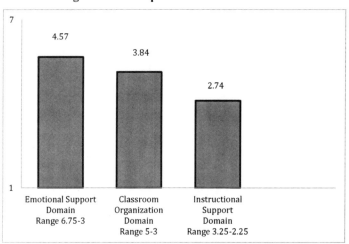

Figure 4.2. Mean scores for Emotional Support Domain, Classroom Organization Domain, and Instructional Support Domain

The CLASS ratings of Nena's curriculum practices (see Figure 4.2) indicated a middle level rating for the Emotional Support Domain (4.57) and for the Classroom Organization Support Domain (3.84), and a low level rating for the Instructional Support Domain (2.74). These ratings were based on mean scores of individual scores assigned to each of the 10 dimensions that comprised the three domains with the highest score assigned to the dimension of positive climate (6.75) and the lowest score assigned to the dimension of quality of feedback (2.25).

Within the domain of Emotional Support, the range of ratings associated with the four individual dimensions varied from a score of 6.75 (positive climate) to a score of 3 (regard for student perspectives). Within the domain of Classroom Organization Support, the range of ratings associated with three individual dimensions varied from a score of 5 (behavior management) to 3 (instructional learning formats). In the domain of Instructional Support, the ratings associated with the three individual dimensions ranged from a score of 3.25 (language modeling) to a score of 2.25 (quality of feedback).

Expansions of educator practices. The atmosphere in Nena's classroom was busy and active. Nena moved around the classroom and paused in various play centers to speak with children as they played. As she spoke with children, she smiled and bent down to their level, welcoming them into the program on a Monday morning. She inquired about weekend activities with their families. Nena offered comfort to a child who was visibly upset when her mother left the center. As the child was crying, Nena gently picked her up and took her to a nearby window inviting her to look for her Mom through the window.

Nena maintained an even and calm voice tone as she communicated with children while she passed through play situations heading to different destinations in the room. Her contact with children was often transitory, and her conversations with them were brief. As she walked through the play room on her way to the art cupboard where she began gathering material for her planned activity, she paused in the block area where two children were playing hockey with mini sticks and commented, "Oh, you are playing hockey, that's great." On another occasion, she walked by a child playing on the computer and paused to inform him that his turn would be over soon.

Nena carried out an activity that involved children painting on tin foil. She prepared the materials, placed the materials in front of her, and invited children to participate by announcing, "If anyone wants to paint on tin foil, come to the table." Several children appeared to be interested and Nena reminded them to put on smocks. She distributed the materials by giving each child a piece of tin foil and asked, "What color would you like to use?" As the children began to paint on the tin foil, Nena

98

focused their attention on the colors they were using by stating, "Look at the color. Is this red? What color do you have now?"

Descriptions of educator beliefs

In explaining her thoughts about curriculum, Nena highlighted the importance of play by stating, "Play is the biggest part of curriculum." She categorized the curriculum approach in her program as being emergent and explained that emergent curriculum to her meant that she could not expect all of the children in her classroom to be interested in the same concept at the same time. She added that emergent curriculum required her to support children as they experienced the program according to their own ideas and plans.

Nena highlighted observation as a key component of emergent curriculum. She explained the importance of observing what the children were doing and using those observations as the source of curriculum. She stated, "It's the children basically guiding us on what they want to learn." She explained that educators had to use observations of children in combination with their own knowledge in order to facilitate and individualize children's learning. Nena illustrated this point by referencing the tinfoil art activity she facilitated earlier with a group of children. She explained her reasoning in offering children tinfoil to paint on and associated it with an observation she recorded the day before. Nena explained that she was curious to see what the children would do if she offered them tin foil to paint on during an activity. As our conversation evolved, Nena excitedly recalled how the activity provided her with an opportunity to teach the children colors, a concept with which they had difficulty. According to her, "They don't even think of it as teaching colors. So, that worked out well."

Nena described the process she and her colleagues followed to generate ideas for curriculum practices. She referred to the weekly planning web that was posted on the bulletin board in the classroom, and explained that from observations of children's play, the educators would determine a major area of interest that became the main curriculum focus. Nena informed me that the current main curriculum focus was winter fun. She reported that in focusing on winter fun, the educators had generated ideas for each area of the classroom and the program. For example, they added mini hockey sticks, hockey jerseys, and hockey socks to the dramatic area; melted snow to make ice chips in the science area; placed big chunks of ice in the sensory bin; made snow castles with children outside; added books about snow and winter in the book area; and provided children with large sheets of paper to print the word snow on in the language area.

Nena expressed some inconsistency in describing her beliefs about what influenced her ideas about the curriculum in her program. While at the start of our conversation she described children's interests as guiding her decisions, as our conversation unfolded, she reported that "what parents would want for their children" was the major source of her curriculum decisions. She explained that when parents would identify to her that their child might be experiencing a challenge with a concept, or if a parent would want their child to learn something specific, such as writing a name, she would say, "Okay, we will work on that."

Nena revealed that for her, making children feel welcome in her program was the most important aspect of curriculum. She extended this idea by explaining how challenging it was for children and parents to be away from each other. Nena reported that "making a home away from home" for the children in her program was one of her most important jobs as an educator.

Nena described the qualities of an effective educator as "patience, understanding, and love for children." She revealed that she became an educator because she loves children and added that she also loves working with the elderly. Nena characterized children and the elderly as similar in that both are dependent on others for their care. She reported that if she were not an educator, she would most likely be working with the elderly.

Nena described her work with the children in her classroom through children's accomplishments and associated those accomplishments with herself. She reported a feeling of satisfaction in teaching the children specific skills that their parents noticed and stated, "It feels so good when you've taught someone something." With delight, she recalled an experience of teaching a preschool child to write her name at the request of the parent. She explained how she guided the child to produce her name through the use of a dot-to-dot process and how pleased the parent was and how good it felt that the parent complimented her.

Nena reported that her curriculum planning process was connected with the provincial document ELECT. She recounted how she referred to the ELECT document to isolate areas of development she would focus on, and skills she would teach to the children, and states, "You want to plan the skills first and think, 'what do I want to work on first with these children'."

In considering how others viewed her work with children, Nena disclosed that being viewed as a teacher was important to her and that individuals who did not view her work as being important frustrated her. Nena described her work as that of teaching skills to the children in her classroom. She explained how when children achieved specific skills she would capture those skills through learning stories on documentation forms to share with the parents. She revealed feeling pleased when parents realized that she was not just babysitting their children and offered her comments, such as "Wow, you guys do a lot, it's not just dropping them off."

Marica

Professional background

Marica is a graduate of a two-year Early Childhood Education recognized college program. During her career, she has worked with children between the ages of two to 12 years and reported that she enjoyed working with all ages. Currently, she works in the preschool program with children between the ages of three to five years.

Marica's employment did not require her to participate in professional development activities. Nevertheless, during her years of working in the field of early education, Marica reported that she participated in numerous professional development experiences. She revealed an interest in learning new information about her profession and in exchanging ideas with other educators from different child-care centers.

During the last year, Marica had attended three separate professional development workshops ranging from two to three hours in length. The three workshops were delivered in the evenings, after working hours, at an off-site location (i.e., a local professional resource center). The decision to attend the workshops was made by Marica and was motivated by her interest in learning new information for her work with children. The topic of the first workshop was early literacy, and the second workshop focused on songs, finger plays, and flannel board stories. Marica described both workshops as "curriculum related," and reported that she gathered many useful ideas that she brought back into her program. The focus of the third workshop was fetal alcohol syndrome. Marica described the workshop as being interesting, but not as meaningful as she had no immediate use for the information that was covered. The fees to attend the three workshops were paid by Marica's workplace.

Curriculum practices

Classroom physical environment and curriculum documents. Marica's program was located in a large hall adjacent to a church building. The hall had been donated to the child-care center by the local church. The entrance to the building lead into a small room that housed cubbies for each child enrolled in the program and a parent bulletin board. The parent bulletin board contained a posted copy of the monthly calendar, the daily schedule of the program, and the weekly program plan. The monthly calendar provided information about special events taking place that month, children's birthdays, and days the center would be closed. The weekly program plan included a listing of the activities that had been planned for that week (see Figure 5.1).

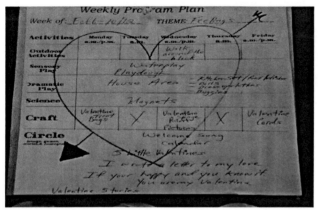

Figure 5.1. The classroom's weekly program plan

Through this room was a doorway leading into a classroom space with three large windows that allowed considerable light to stream into the space. The classroom space was divided into play centers that were located around the edge of the room. The play centers included a writing area, art area, block area, dress-up area, book area, and a circle area. Located in the middle of the room was a large adult-sized table with bench seating, a large plastic dollhouse, and child-sized tables with chairs around them, used for meal times and group activities.

The play centers in the classroom included materials that were organized and arranged for easy access by children (see Figure 5.2). The classroom walls were decorated with commercial posters and alphabet letter cut outs. On the day of the observation, there was no evidence of child created art on any classroom walls.

Figure 5.2. Organized materials for easy access by children

CLASS ratings of educator practices.

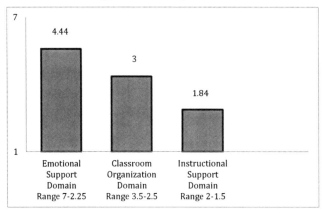

Figure 5.3. Mean scores for Emotional Support Domain, Classroom Organization Domain, and Instructional Support Domain

The CLASS ratings of Marica's curriculum practices (see Figure 5.3) indicated a middle level rating for the Emotional Support Domain (4.44) and for the Classroom Organization Support Domain (3), and a low level rating for the Instructional Support Domain (1.84). These ratings were based on mean scores of individual scores assigned to each of the 10 dimensions that comprised the three domains with the highest score assigned to the inverted rating for the dimension of negative climate (7) and the lowest score assigned to the dimension of concept development (1.5).

Within the domain of Emotional Support, the range of ratings associated with the four individual dimensions varied from a score of 7 (negative climate) to a score of 2.25 (regard for student perspectives). Within the domain of Classroom Organization Support, the range of ratings associated with three individual dimensions varied from a score of 3.5 (productivity) to 2.5 (behavior management). In the domain of Instructional Support, the ratings associated with the three individual dimensions ranged from a score of 2 (language modeling; quality of feedback) to a score of 1.5 (concept development).

Expansions of educator practices. The atmosphere in the classroom was calm and quiet as the children were playing in various parts of the room. Marica moved around the classroom and joined various groups of children while they played.

Marica's interactions with the children in her program were warm and genuine. When she spoke with children, she got down to their physical level, smiled and made eye contact with them. She shared her experiences with the children of travelling to the child care centre and invited them into a conversation. The children reciprocated by commenting and adding their own information. While interacting with a group of children in the block area, Marica guided their play through questions, such as, "What will hold up the roof?" or, "What shape are you using?" or, "What's missing on the side of the house?" or through directions, such as, "Put them over there. Let's build the wall around so you can stand over here."

Marica carried out a circle time activity that focused on the calendar. She pointed to a large calendar located beside her and asked the children the name of the month. When she did not receive an answer, she provided the name for that month. Marica extended by asking the children if Groundhog Day had passed yet. As there was no answer from the children, she informed them, that yes it had passed. Marica and the children sang a song about the days of the week and when they finished Marica focused

105

the children's attention on the number five on the calendar and asked the children to tell her what number comes next. When the children did not reply Marica made a sound "s" for the next letter and offered the word "six." This activity continued as Marica provided the name for the day of the week and followed up by asking the children to repeat it with her. Following this, Marica invited the children to tell her what day tomorrow will be and what day yesterday was. The children shouted out names for the days of the week after each question and Marica praised them when they provided the right answer.

Descriptions of educator beliefs

In disclosing the reasoning behind her curriculum decisions, Marica emphasized the importance of ensuring that the children in her program were prepared for school. She directed my attention to the writing area that had been set up in the classroom that included nameplates for each child so they could begin tracing their names. She explained that she was introduced to these ideas at workshops she attended years before and that the ideas were based on two commercial literacy programs. When I probed for additional information about these two programs, Marica did not offer much detail. She explained that she has heard that the local kindergarten teachers used the same programs in their classrooms.

Figure 5.4. The writing area

During our conversation, I inquired if the children had additional opportunities in the program to engage in writing. Marica advised me that at one of the workshops she attended this past year the presenters had suggested introducing materials such as clipboards, menus, and writing tools, into play areas so that children could engage in writing through play. She revealed that she still had to add those materials to the classroom.

Marica categorized her curriculum approach as being theme-based. She explained that she preferred themes because they offered her direction and made it clear as to what to speak to children about. Marica recognized that many of her colleagues were changing their approach to curriculum to be more consistent with an emergent curriculum, but insisted that she was "old school," and that she was going to continue with themes because, "…that is how I was taught as an ECE."

As our conversation unfolded, Marica revealed that circle time was her favorite time of the day to engage the children in learning. She acknowledged that if the opportunity arose to highlight concepts, such as colors and numbers during free-play, she would seize it; however, she added, "When you sit down for circle time, I've got their attention… and I can give them my information that I have."

Marica described effective educators as caring and patient individuals who had good organization skills and communicated well with parents. She revealed that she became an educator because she loved working with children and their families. Marica reported that she believed the parents of the children in her program viewed her work as important and that they were grateful to her for her work in teaching their children skills needed for school.

In considering how others who were not associated with her program viewed her work as an educator, Marica reported that their views would be negative and stated, "There's still a lot of people that see us as glorified babysitters." Marica stated that being viewed as a glorified babysitter was the most frustrating aspect of her work as an educator. She noted that educators should be valued because they are engaged in valuable work and added, "We are professional even though we may not be working in the [school] board; we are educating as well."

In expanding on her thoughts about the contribution educators made to children's learning, Marica offered a comparison between elementary teachers working in the school system and educators working in child-care. She stated, "We [educators] are not sitting down at tables doing writing all the time with children, and that's changing in the school board because they are doing play-based all day learning." Marica's final thoughts drifted into hopefulness about recognition of educators' work in the future. She shared her belief that as early childhood principles and play-based learning made their way into the school system, the view of educators as professionals would increase.

Cross Case Analysis

The following section presents recurring themes across all case studies followed by an analysis of those themes. Reoccurring themes are categorized into three types: dominant themes, strong themes, and weak themes. Dominant themes are those for which all five participants exhibit the same or similar characteristic, implement the same or similar practice, and provide the same or similar response. Strong themes are those for which four participants exhibit the same or similar characteristic, implement the same or similar practice, and provide the same or similar response. Weak themes are those for which two or three participants exhibit the same or similar characteristic, implement the same or similar practice, and provide the same or similar response. The reporting of recurring themes is structured around the following categories: professional background of participants (professional qualifications; professional development), curriculum practices (classroom physical environment and curriculum documents; CLASS ratings of educator practices; expansions of educator practices), descriptions of educators' beliefs about curriculum, and descriptions of educators' professional identity.

I present four tables and two charts summarizing the recurring themes across all cases for each of the categories: emerging themes related to professional background of participants including professional qualifications and professional development experiences (see Table 1); emerging themes related to curriculum practices including classroom physical environment and curriculum documents (see Table 2); mean scores of CLASS ratings for the domains of Emotional Support, Classroom Organization Support, and Instructional Support (see Figure 6); mean scores of individual dimensions with the domains of Emotional Support, Classroom Organization, and Instructional Support (see Figure 8); emerging themes related to expansions of curriculum practices (see Table 3); emerging themes related to descriptions of beliefs about curriculum (see Table 4); and emerging themes related to descriptions of beliefs about professional identity (see Table 5). Lastly, I provide a more complete description of those emerging themes and chart rating summaries.

Emerging themes of professional background of participants

Eight themes (six dominant themes and two strong themes) surrounding the dimension of professional background emerge among the participants of this study (see Table 1). Two of these themes (one dominant theme and one strong theme) are related to professional qualifications of participating educators and six of these themes (five dominant themes and one strong theme) are related to the professional development experiences of the participating educators.

Professional qualifications. The first theme to emerge related to professional qualifications is a dominant theme indicating that all five participants attended a recognized post-secondary college to obtain the credential required for working in a licensed child-care center. The second theme to emerge is a strong theme indicating that a diploma in Early Childhood Education is the highest credential attained for four participating educators.

Table 1

Emerging Themes Related to the Professional Backgrounds of Participants

	Emerging Themes
Dominant themes	1. Participants attended a recognized college program to obtain the required credential for working in a licensed child-care center (5/5).
	2. Participants reported learning information through workshops attended during the last year that was immediately useful to their practices(5/5).
	3. Participants worked for organizations that support staff participation in all and any professional development by reimbursing at least 50% of all associated fees (5/5).
	4. Participants reported that ongoing professional development was important to their work as educators (5/5).
	5. Participants reported attending at least three separate professional development activities during the last year (5/5).
Strong Themes	6. Participants reported attending at least one workshop described as "curriculum related" during the last year (5/5).
	7. Diploma in Early Childhood Education is the highest credential attained by participatns (4/5).
	8. Participants reported being fully (100%) reimbursed for attending workshops during the last year (4/5).

The decision made by the participants in this study to attend community college in order to obtain the credentials required to work in a licensed child-care center is consistent with the educational backgrounds of the early childhood education workforce in Ontario. Tabulations from 2001 Canadian census data indicate that 78.6% of educators working in licensed child-care centers in Ontario were in possession of the education credential required by the province to grant the center a license to operate (Beach et al., 2009). Of those, 65.9% had obtained the required credential through a college program (Beach et al., 2009).

The same census data reveal that only 12.7% of the 78.6% of early childhood qualified workforce in Ontario had obtained a bachelor degree or higher. This statistic is consistent with the low number of participants in this study, one out of five, who reported having credentials higher than a diploma (Beach et al., 2009).

Professional development. The third theme to emerge is a dominant theme indicating that all five participants worked for organizations that support staff participation in staff-initiated professional development by reimbursing at least 50% of all associated fees. A fourth theme to emerge is a strong theme in that four participating educators reported that they were fully reimbursed for attending curriculum-related workshops that focused on strengthening their knowledge of the emergent curriculum approach. The emergence of these two themes indicates strong support by the child-care center administration for staff professional development in general, and a commitment to implementing emergent curriculum, in particular. Research in Canada has identified the cost of professional development as a systematic barrier that prevents early childhood educators from accessing current knowledge and information related to their field (Beach, Bertrand, Forer, Michal, & Tougas, 2004). This barrier has been removed for the educators participating in this study.

The next four themes to emerge are dominant themes reported by all five participants related to other aspects of educator participation in professional development: (1) On-going professional development is important to their work as educators; (2) they attended at least three separate professional development activities during the last year; (3) they learned information through professional development that was immediately useful to their practice; and (4) at least one workshop attended during the last year was "curriculum related." The emergence of these dominant themes indicates that the educators who participated in this study placed a high value on participating in professional development. All five educators reported that they participated in at least three separate professional development experiences during the past year.

The professional development experiences reported by the educators who participated in this study are consistent with professional development participation rates across Ontario, as research data indicate that 79.8% of child-care center staff working in licensed centers participated in some form of professional development during the course of a 12-month period (Beach et al., 2004). In addition to participating in three separate professional development experiences during the past year, each of the five participants described the professional development experience as being positive and useful. Each of the five participants recalled specific details that had been shared through professional development that they were able to use immediately in their practices. Finally, the participants placed a high value on strengthening their knowledge of emergent curriculum by choosing to attend professional development related to this topic.

Combined, all of these elements present a portrait of the participants of this study as qualified educators who worked in supportive organizations that promoted emergent curriculum through ongoing professional development of staff. In addition, they presented themselves as educators who were genuinely interested in and committed to ongoing professional learning in general, and in ongoing professional learning related to emergent curriculum, in particular. These educators indicated that they sought out

112

professional development opportunities that would strengthen and expand their knowledge and enhance their practices.

Emerging themes of curriculum practices

Classroom physical environment and curriculum documents. Five recurring themes emerged in association with classroom physical environment and curriculum documents (see Table 2). The first three of these themes are classified as dominant themes that were observed in all five participating classrooms, one theme is classified as strong as it was observed in four participating classrooms, and one theme is classified as weak as it was observed in three participating classrooms.

The first emerging theme was a dominant one related to classroom set-up and reflected the curriculum practice of arranging the physical space into play centers. The types of play centers of each classroom were similar and included a block area, art area, dress-up area, library and book area, and sand and water area.

The second emerging theme, also a dominant theme related to classroom set-up, was the inclusion of interesting materials within the play centers. These materials were open-ended materials such as blocks, toilet paper rolls, and lego, that could be used in various ways by children and that did not, by their design, limit children's imagination or creativity. In addition, these materials were clearly labeled through the use of pictures and symbols, and were easily accessible to children.

The third emerging theme was the inclusion of posted activities that had been planned for that week. This theme, a dominant one, was observed as a curriculum practice among all five participating educators. The listings of upcoming weekly activities were posted in prominent locations in the classroom and could be easily viewed by parents and other visitors to the classroom.

The next theme to emerge was observed as a curriculum practice among four participating educators and is classified as a strong theme. This curriculum practice included the postings of documentations around the classroom. These documentations were in the form of panels and forms that included pictures of children involved in various activities and descriptions of children's learning.

The last emerging theme included the curriculum practice of posting a Brainstorming Form on the walls of the classroom that was designed to record observations of children's interests. This theme was observed among the curriculum practices of three of the participating educators and is classified as a weak theme.

Table 2

Emerging Themes Related to Classroom Physical Environment and Curriculum Documents

	Emerging Themes
Dominant themes	1. Classroom space arranged into play centers that include block area, art area, dress-up area, library and book area, and sand and water tables (5/5).
	2. Play centers that included open-ended materials that were organized, labeled and accessible to children (5/5).
Strong theme	3. Listings of activities planned for that week posted in the classroom (5/5).
Weak theme	4. Documentations of children's learning posted around the classroom (4/5).
	5. Brainstorming Form designed to record observations of children's interests posted in the classroom (3/5).

Emerging themes of CLASS ratings of educator practices.

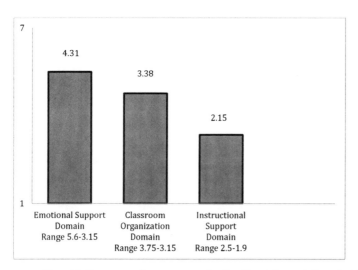

Figure 6. Summary of mean scores for Emotional Support Domain, Classroom Organization Domain, and Instructional Support Domain

Figure 6 presents the mean scores across all cases for the domains of Emotional Support, Classroom Organization, and Instructional Support. Figure 7 presents the mean scores across all cases for the individual dimensions within each of the three domains.

The Emotional Support Domain includes the dimensions of negative climate (NC), positive climate (PC), teacher sensitivity (TS), and regard for student perspectives (RSP). The Classroom Organization Domain includes the dimensions of productivity (PD), behavior management (BM), and instructional learning formats (ILF). The Instructional Support Domain includes the dimensions of language modeling (LM), quality of feedback (QF), and concept development (CD).

Summary of mean scores of CLASS ratings for three domains. The highest mean score among the three domains is associated with the Emotional Support Domain (4.31). This domain is comprised of four separate dimensions with mean scores that

115

range from an inverted 5.6 (negative climate) to 3.15 (regard for student perspectives). This overall domain rating indicates that among the curriculum practices expressed by the participants in this study, there was little evidence of there being a negative climate with only mild frequencies and mild levels of negative behaviors such as sarcasm, disrespect, punitive control, and negativity expressed by educators and children; that there was some evidence of emotional connections between educators and children and among children through warmth, respect, and verbal and non-verbal interactions; that there was some evidence of teacher sensitivity through awareness, responsiveness, addressing of problems that came up, and comforting of children; and that there was some evidence of educators' emphasizing children's interests and points of view in order to encourage responsibility and independence.

The second highest mean score among the three domains is for the Classroom Organization Domain (3.38). This domain includes three separate dimensions with mean scores ranging from 3.75 (productivity) to 3.15 (instructional learning supports). This overall domain rating indicates that most of the time during the day the educators who participated in this study managed instructional time and routines well; however, there was evidence of some lost learning time as educators dealt with disruptions and completed routine tasks during play-time.

The lowest mean score among the three domains is for the Instructional Support Domain (2.15). This domain has three separate dimensions with mean scores from 2.5 (language modeling) to 1.9 (concept development). This overall domain rating indicates that the educators who participated in this study rarely engaged in curriculum practices that promoted children's deep understanding of concepts and higher-order thinking through effective feedback and language modeling.

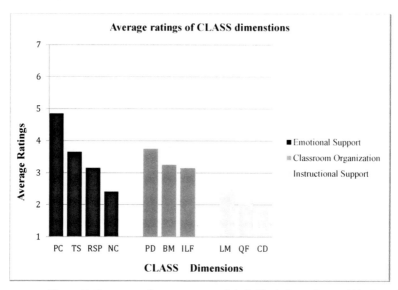

Figure 7. Summary of mean scores of individual dimensions within Emotional Support Domain, Classroom Organization Domain, and Instructional Support Domain

Individual dimension ratings within the Emotional Support Domain. The strongest dimension within the Emotional Support Domain is positive climate (PC) with a mean score of 4.85. This rating indicates that the educators and the children participated in some activities together; that there were some social conversations between educators and children and among children; and that there was some co-operation and sharing between educators and children. This rating also indicates that there were some displays of smiling, laughter, verbal and physical affection and that there were some demonstrations of a warm and respectful tone as educators communicated with children.

The next strongest dimension is teacher sensitivity (TS) with a mean score of 3.65. This rating indicates that the educators sometimes noticed children's lack of understanding, anticipated problems and planned for them accordingly. It also indicates that educators were sometimes responsive to children's needs by acknowledging emotions and by providing comfort and assistance, while at other times they were dismissive of and unresponsive to children's needs and interests. Finally, this rating reveals that the children sometimes sought guidance and support from educators and sometimes shared their ideas with educators freely.

The next strongest dimension within the Emotional Support Domain was assigned to the dimension of regard for student perspectives (RSP), with a mean score of 3.15. This rating indicates that while educators followed children's leads some of the time, they were more controlling at other times. It also indicates that the educators provided support for children to take leadership and to express their ideas for some tasks, but retained control, limiting child expression, and restricted physical movements of children at other times.

The weakest rating within the Emotional Support Domain was assigned to the negative climate dimension (NC). With a mean score of 2.4, this rating indicates that the curriculum practices demonstrated by the educator participants in this study included only mild and infrequent displays of irritability, anger, and use of harsh voice tone that may have contributed to peer aggression and negativity within the classroom.

Individual dimension ratings within the Classroom Organization Domain. The strongest dimension within the Classroom Organization Domain was productivity (PD) with a mean score of 3.75. This indicates that the educators were prepared for activities that were carried out most of the time, but did leave children's learning time to take care of some preparation. It also indicates there were too many transitions within the program that took too long, leaving children wandering around the classroom or uncertain as to what was expected of them.

The next strongest dimension is behavior management (BM) with a mean score of 3.25. This score indicates that there was an inconsistency in the use of effective behaviour management practices among the educators participating in this study. While classroom rules and expectations were clearly stated, they were not consistently enforced or followed up, and while educators used a balance of proactive and reactive strategies, these were not implemented consistently, thereby contributing to periodic episodes of misbehavior.

The third dimension within the Organizational Support Domain is instructional learning formats (ILF) with a mean score of 3.15. This score indicates that the educators were inconsistent in their involvement with children during the program and in expanding children's interests through the use of effective questions, a range of modalities (auditory; sensory; visual; movement), interesting materials, and hands-on opportunities. This score also indicates that children were sometimes interested and engaged in what was going on in the program, but at other times they were not interested or engaged.

Individual dimension ratings within the Instructional Support Domain. The strongest dimension within the Instructional Support Domain is language modeling (LM) with a mean score of 2.5. This score indicates that few conversations were observed between children and educators and among children that included back and forth exchanges contingent on responding. It also reveals that the majority of educators' questions were close-ended questions requiring right/wrong, or one-word responses. Educators rarely mapped actions with language or introduced advanced language by connecting unfamiliar words to a familiar idea as a way to facilitate language stimulation.

The next strongest dimension is quality of feedback (QF) with a mean score of 2.05. This score indicates that there were rare occurrences where educators queried children or provided hints or assistance to assist them in explaining their thinking. This score also indicates that the educators rarely offred additional information to children and that they mostly provided perfunctory feedback to children during exchanges.

The last dimension within the Instructional Support Domain is concept development (CD) with a mean score of 1.9. This score reveals that the educators rarely encouraged children in analysis and reasoning through "why" and "how" questions, opportunities to predict and test ideas, and compare and evaluate ideas. This score also

119

indicates that educators presented concepts and ideas independent of each other, rarely engaging children to integrate ideas with previous knowledge and experiences, or with their actual lived experiences.

Expansions of educator practices. An expanded analysis of the observational data of all five participants reveals three additional strong emerging themes related to curriculum practices (see Table 3).

Table 3

Emerging Themes Related to Expansions of Educator Practices

	Emerging Themes
Dominant themes	1. Participants physically moved to locations associated with children's play activities during free-play time (5/5).
	2. Participants emphasized academic concepts of letter, number, color, and calendar recognition through the program (5/5).
Strong theme	3. Participants carried out planned activities that were not connected with direct observations of children's prior interest in the activity focus (4/5).

The first theme to emerge is a dominant theme that highlighted the curriculum practice of physically moving around the classroom during free-play to locations associated with children's play activities. All five participants demonstrated considerable physical movement among play centers inside the classroom and among playground equipment outside the classrooms in order to locate themselves close to children's play activities.

The second dominant theme to emerge revealed curriculum practices that emphasized academic concepts of letter, number, color, and calendar recognition. All five educators demonstrated these practices throughout their programs as they highlighted letter, number, color, or calendar recognition while interacting with the children. At times, this emphasis was expressed during the free-play portion of the program as educators initiated verbal communications, such as "What color are you using?" or "How many blocks do you have?" to direct children's attention to a particular focus occurring in play. At other times, this emphasis occurred as a result of educators' planned activities that they carried out. Three educators carried out planned activities surrounding academic concepts; two highlighted individual letters; while a third devoted a circle time activity to engaging the children in calendar time and memorizing days of the week. Finally, a fourth educator who planned an activity to allow children to explore the qualities of tin-foil in response to an observed interest dominated the activity with a focus on naming the colors the children were using and on eliciting color names from them.

The third theme to emerge was a strong theme that revealed participating educators carried out planned activities that were not connected with direct observations of children's prior interest. These educators planned and implemented activities that were motivated by sources external to the interests of the children. One participant planned and implemented an activity based on a prepackaged language program introduced by someone else, another implemented an activity around the letter of the week, a third participant implemented an activity sourced from a predetermined craft associated with the theme of Christmas, and a fourth participant implemented an activity that focused on the name of the month and days of the week associated with the calendar. Three of these participants posted a brainstorming form in their classrooms that had been designed to record the interests of the children in the program for the purpose of generating future curriculum ideas. Each form revealed incomplete recordings of children's interests.

Emerging themes of educators' beliefs about curriculum

The same observational data used to produce ratings of curriculum practices were utilized to inspire interview questions with each participant. The strategy of referencing specific curriculum observations in which the participants engaged only hours before each interview allowed for deeper, more authentic discussions during the interview process.

Five patterns emerged across all cases in association with descriptions of curriculum beliefs; three of these were strong themes reported by four educators and two were weak themes reported by three educators (see Table 4). The first strong pattern to emerge was the emphasis of play as an important part of curriculum. Four participants described play as an essential vehicle for engaging children in learning. These participants emphasized that children learn many important concepts through play and highlighted the importance of engaging with children during play.

Table 4

Emerging Themes Related to Descriptions of Curriculum Beliefs

	Emerging Themes
Strong themes	1. Emphasized play as an important part of curriculum (4/5).
	2. Identified children's ideas as essential to emergent curriculum (4/5).
	3. Identified observations of children's interests as source for planned activities (4/5).
Weak Themes	
	4. Children are capable (3/5).
·	5. Identified curriculum approach being followed as emergent (3/5).

The second strong theme to emerge was the participants' reported beliefs that the implementation of emergent curriculum required them to follow children's ideas as the guide to curriculum decisions. Four participants explained that to them implementing emergent curriculum meant an expectation that "not all the children are interested in the same idea at the same time." These participants emphasized the role of children's ideas and interests as the inspiration for their curriculum practices.

The third strong theme to emerge was reported by four participants and included the belief that observations of children's interests were the source of their planned activities. Three of these participants pointed to specific forms posted in their programs that they used to record these observations.

In addition to these strong themes, two weak themes reported by three participants emerged in association with descriptions of curriculum beliefs. The first of these, children are capable, emerged as a result of two opposing views that were threaded through conversations with participants: the view that children are capable and the view that children are dependent on educators for their learning. As they explained the reasoning for using observations of children's interests as their guide for curriculum decisions, three participants exposed the view that children are capable. These three participants described the interests of the children in their program with delight, and in conversation with me, attributed significance to these interests. In an attempt to convince me of this significance, one participant stated, "You would be amazed at how much information they have."

The opposing view, children are dependent on educators for learning, was exposed through stories recalled by three participants. One participant revealed that circle time is her favorite time of the day as during that time the children are all sitting and listening to her, and she can give them the information they need to learn. The second participant exposed this opposing view as she recalled an incident involving children having difficulty in deciding who would be first in a line-up. She explained that she brought closure to this incident by stating, "We're not having a leader." The same participant described her method of teaching children to socialize well with others. She accomplished this by determining the maximum number of children who could be present in each play center. She communicated this assigned number by posting pictorial outlines of children in each play center, and monitored children's play to ensure they were following this directive. She justified this strategy by stating, "Sometimes all of the children want to be in the same area at the same time, and that causes conflict." A third participant characterized children and the elderly to be alike in that both groups depend on others for their care.

The second weak theme to emerge was the participants' reported belief that they were following an emergent curriculum approach. Three participants directly labeled their approach as emergent curriculum.

Emerging themes of educators' descriptions of professional identity

Four recurring patterns in relation to educators' descriptions of professional identity were noted. One of these patterns emerged as a dominant theme that was reported by all five participant educators and three emerged as strong themes that were reported by four participants (see Table 5). The first theme to emerge in association with descriptions of professional identity was the dominant theme of relinquishing significant curriculum decisions to others. Two participants used prepackaged literacy activities that had been recommended by elementary school teachers who did not work in their programs. Two participants attributed their approach to documentation to a workshop leader who provided them with a template to fill in, a process that one identified as liking because it was so easy. Another participant described how a curriculum directive from an expert consultant resulted in helping the children in her program socialize well with others by reducing conflict. This curriculum directive instructed her to produce picture outlines of the number of children she desired to be in each play area and to monitor that the children did not exceed that number. In describing this directive, the educator did not provide any evidence that she made modifications to the directive provided in order to suit the characteristics of her program. Another participant explained that her curriculum decisions were influenced by what parents told her that they wanted their children to learn. She recalled a story of how she taught a young child to write her name following the parent's request.

The second theme to emerge was that of educator as being loving, patient, and caregiving. In describing their thoughts about qualities associated with being an effective educator, four participants made references to the importance of educators having patience and understanding in order to work with young children. Each of these four educators highlighted a love of children as their reasoning for becoming educators.

Table 5

Emerging Themes Associated with Descriptions of Professional Identity

	Emerging Themes
Dominant theme	1. Educators relinquishing significant curriculum decisions to others (5/5).
Strong themes	2. Educator as loving, patient, and caregiving (4/5).
	3. Educators' views that their work with children is misunderstood and undervalued by society (4/5).
	4. Educators teaching skills to children that are valued by others (4/5).

The third theme to emerge related to descriptions of professional identity is a strong theme that pointed to a reported view that the work of early childhood educators is misunderstood and undervalued by society. Four participants described their beliefs that others label their work as babysitting, a label they highlighted as being the most frustrating aspect of their work.

The fourth strong theme to emerge among participants was an apparent necessity to be validated for teaching skills to children that are valued by others. Two participants revealed that they posted documentation forms on the walls of their classrooms to communicate to parents that they are teaching valuable skills to the children and that these postings resulted in positive attention of their work by the parents. A third participant recalled a story of a child who sat her parents in front of her at home and pretended to carry out a circle just like she does. She described her pleasure at how this event demonstrated to the parents that she was teaching important skills to the children in her program. A fourth participant expressed delight in being praised by a parent for teaching a child to write her name at that parent's request. The participant described that she accomplished this by employing a hand-over-hand technique as the child was demonstrating difficulty in producing the letters on her own.

Chapter 5: Discussion

The purpose of this study was to examine the inter-relationships among curriculum practices, beliefs about curriculum and professional identity of educators. The use of a mixed method research design provided reliable data of educators' practices through observations of those practices. Complementary to those data, additional information (photographs of classroom environments; collections of curriculum documents; and interviews) gathered through conversations with individual participants presented context-specific profiles of each participants' experiences, understandings and evolving beliefs that have been documented.

Using all of these data, the five case studies have been analyzed for emerging themes within each case, and across all cases. The qualitative nature of this approach does not presume to offer definitive conclusions or causal relationships among these phenomena; rather it provides descriptions and interpretations of emerging themes in order to gain a deeper and more complete understanding of the relationships among curriculum practices, beliefs about curriculum and professional identity.

In this section, I present an analysis and interpretation of the findings uncovered through this study. First, by drawing on the emerging themes presented in the previous chapter, I answer each of the questions posed by this study and offer analysis and interpretation of the responses. Next, through consideration and reflection, I draw on the literature and research associated with this topic, in order to formulate an explanation that describes the inter-relationship of curriculum practices, curriculum beliefs, and professional identities of early childhood educators working in licensed child-care settings in Ontario.

The main research question guiding this study is: What are the relationships among beliefs about curriculum, curriculum practices, and professional identities in qualified early childhood educators? Before I undertake this central research question, I will respond to the following secondary questions that have been inspired by the main research question:

1) What are qualified early childhood educators' curriculum practices?
2) What are qualified early childhood educators' self-reported beliefs about curriculum?
3) How do qualified early childhood educators describe their professional identity?
4) What are the relations among educational and professional backgrounds of qualified early childhood educators and their self-reported beliefs about curriculum, their practices of curriculum, and their descriptions of professional identity?

What are qualified early childhood educators' curriculum practices?

To fully answer this question, it is important to consider what curriculum practices are, how they are described, and what influences their expression in a classroom setting. In early childhood education, curriculum practices have been described as expressions of curriculum frameworks (Bennett, 2005; Katz, 1999) that are profoundly influenced by educators' understandings and personal commitments to these frameworks (Kagan, 1992; Marcon, 2002).

Curriculum practices are all experiences, activities, and events that take place during the day that contribute to children's learning (Goffin, 1994). They include the following elements: classroom physical space; design, implementation, and evaluation of learning experiences; nature of engaging with children during play time; method of dealing with conflict situations among children; manner of engaging with parents in the program; and method of documenting children's learning and program events (Goffin, 1994; Stacey, 2009). These practices do not take place in a vacuum. They are carried out within the context of a classroom environment that is defined by the emotional atmosphere and the organizational flow of the classroom that are both influenced by these practices and that stimulate their presence and quality (Chaille, 2008; Curtis & Carter, 2008; Dietze & Kashin, 2012; Stacey, 2009).

The findings of this study reveal that the educators engaged in a combination of instructivist-inspired and constructivist-inspired curriculum practices. This finding is consistent with early childhood literature that describes educators' practices as falling within a continuum of constructivist-inspired practices in that some of their practices may be more inspired by constructivism than are other practices (Chaille, 2008). These findings further reveal that the dominant and strong constructivist-inspired practices demonstrated by these educators were related to the arrangement of their physical classroom space, the presence of documentation and their movements around the classroom during free-play time; their dominant and strong instructivist-inspired curriculum practices were related to guiding children's learning during free-play and planned experiences, and the inspiration behind their planned experiences. In addition, findings reveal that a particular clustering of demonstrated practices served to define the classroom's emotional and organizational atmospheres as moderate and set the tone for the expression of additional practises associated with guiding children's learning.

Participating educators demonstrated constructivist-inspired practices as they organized classroom spaces into play centers (block area, an art area, dress-up area, library and book area, and sand and water tables) that included a variety of open-ended materials (blocks, toilet paper rolls, Lego, etc.,), that were well organized, clearly labeled (pictures; outlines of materials; and written language), and easily accessible to children. These practices, evidenced through two dominant themes, proved to be the strongest expressions of a constructivist-inspired framework among all of the curriculum practices demonstrated by the educators.

This feature is similar to other study findings that revealed consistently higher ratings of educators' room arrangement practices than other curriculum practices (Burchinal, Cryer, Clifford, & Howes, 2002; Doherty et al., 2000). A research study

129

investigating quality in Canadian child-care centers through the use of the Early Childhood Environment Rating Scale-Revised (ECERS-R) (Harms, Clifford, & Cryer, 1998) collected data from 142 non-profit, licensed child-care centers across Canada staffed by educators who held a diploma in Early Childhood Education. ECERS-R is an environment assessment tool consisting of 43 items that provide ratings among seven dimensions of structure quality: space and furnishings; personal care routines; language and reasoning; activities; interaction; program structure; and parents and staff. Each item was scored on a seven-point scale of quality from 1 (inadequate) to 7 (excellent) based on classroom observation and staff interviews. Study findings revealed that classrooms staffed by educators who held a diploma in Early Childhood Education received a mean rating of 5 for space and furnishings and a mean rating of 4.1 for learning activities (Doherty et al., 2000).

The strength behind participating educators' room arrangement practices may be associated with their professional training and the straightforward nature of arranging and equipping a classroom. All five participating educators had graduated from a two-year professional training program that most likely introduced them to a number of textbooks detailing constructivist-inspired ideas and strategies for classroom design. It may be that these practices are simpler to learn through professional training as they often involve defined strategies and classroom checklists than practices associated with guiding children's learning. It may be that a suitable classroom design is easy to achieve by replicating ideas and pictures found in textbooks. On the other hand, practices associated with guiding children's learning are seldom presented in textbooks as defined strategies that can be easily replicated. Rather, they are described as possibilities that depend on interpretations of a number of complex variables where implementation requires professional decision-making.

While all five of these educators demonstrated constructivist-inspired practices in relation to their classroom organization (Jacobs et al., 2007; Dietze & Kashin, 2012; Epstein, 2007), it is worthy of mention that the Ontario licensing regulations

130

associated with classroom organization complement constructivist-inspired strategies (*Day Nurseries Act*, R.S.O., 1990). It may be that these educators' room arrangement practices may, in part, be inspired by the necessity of conforming to these regulations.

The next curriculum practice demonstrated by four of these educators was that of posting documentations around the classroom. Inspired by a constructivist framework, documentations are representations of classroom experiences that make children's learning visible (Jacobs et al., 2007; Curtis & Carter, 2008; Stacey, 2009). They take the form of pictures, drawings, or three-dimensional creations that are combined with dictations of children's language or children's own writing. Posted documentations reflect the belief that children's experiences are valued by the classroom community and invite children and educators to revisit ideas and concepts for the purpose of digging deeper and collaborating in a process of meaning making and co-construction of knowledge (Curtis & Carter, 2008).

These four participating educators may have demonstrated the use of documentations as a result of having engaged in professional development during the last year that introduced them to emergent curriculum. They revealed that they attended workshops that outlined documentation strategies as a component of emergent curriculum and that these strategies were useful to their immediate practices. One educator participating in this study did not demonstrate the use of documentation in her program. That same educator described her approach to curriculum as being theme-based rather than emergent. That same educator did not report attending workshops that focused specifically on this topic. As a result of her theme-based approach to curriculum, she may not have chosen to engage in professional development that would introduce her to documentation or to implement documentation practices in her program.

In order to gain a fuller understanding of the motivations behind this demonstrated curriculum practice among the four participating educators, it may be helpful to consider the format followed in practicing the use of documentations. Two educators created documentation panels that included pictures of children's experiences accompanied by

131

written language that described those experiences. One of the educators posted the panels in the classroom at a level that children could see and the other educator posted the panels in the hallway entering the classroom on the parent bulletin board. Two other educators used documentation forms that resembled a handout to be filled in that included a space for a picture, a space for a written description of the experience and a space that detailed the skills learned by participating children. Both of these educators posted the documentation forms at adult height, with one educator posting them on the classroom door under a heading *Look What We Are Learning*. In addition, two educators revealed through our interview conversations that the reason behind their posting of documentations was associated with attempting to communicate to parents the valuable skills they are teaching the children. This closer examination revealed that perhaps these educators' motivation to use documentation for the purpose of making the value of their work visible to parents may have eclipsed their motivation of making children's learning visible to the classroom community as promoted by a constructivist-inspired framework. It may also be that they did not fully understand the constructivist-inspired principles associated with the use of documentation in order to engage children more fully in learning.

In addition to these curriculum practices, all five educators posted a description of their upcoming weekly planned activities in a prominent location in the classroom as a method of communicating with parents and other visitors to the classroom what the curriculum focus would be for that week. This practice is a requirement of the provincial licensing regulations (*Day Nurseries Act,* R.S.O., 1990) and may be the motivating factor behind this observed practice. However, the provincial licensing regulations do not dictate the format to be followed in expressing these descriptions, and a further examination of each format may offer a deeper understanding of this curriculum practice.

In expressing future curriculum plans in their programs, two participating educators included postings that listed only names of the activities that would be

132

implemented. Through this practice, these educators met the minimum licensing requirement. Three additional educators included postings that demonstrated the use of a curriculum web format that expressed upcoming activity descriptions within a context of other activities in which the children engaged during that week. However, one of these curriculum web postings was incomplete.

The use of a curriculum web as a method of describing upcoming activities is a common curriculum practice promoted by a constructivist-inspired framework (Curtis & Carter, 2008; Stacey, 2009). The demonstration of this practice by only three educators, with one implementing it in an incomplete format, may be associated with their condition of transitioning into emergent curriculum, a condition that was noted by these three participants. It may be that in order to fully transition from merely listing activity names to describing upcoming activities within a context of other curriculum experiences, these educators require additional professional development support. It may also be that the type of professional development they require is other than two-hour workshops in which they participated. They may require on-site consultations that connect classroom observations more intentionally with on-going learning, a professional development approach that has been recommended by professional development literature as a more sound strategy in facilitating educators' fuller understanding and integration of constructivist-inspired principles into their practices (Howe et al., 2012; Riley & Roach, 2006).

An additional curriculum practice demonstrated by all five educators was the practice of physically locating themselves in areas where children were playing during the free-play portion of the day. This practice revealed a high value for play as an important element of curriculum. Professionals who have outlined positive educator interactions through their writing have identified educators' need to locate themselves in areas where children are playing as a constructivist-inspired curriculum practice (Curtis & Carter, 2008; Chaille, 2008; Jacobs et al., 2007). Participating educators may have gained a heightened awareness of play through their exposure to the provincial curriculum framework ELECT (Ministry of Children and Youth Services, 2006). The ELECT document devotes considerable attention to describing play as an important aspect of children's curriculum. All five educators indicated that they were exposed to this document and its writings through their place of employment or through the workshops that they attended. Perhaps, the curriculum framework influenced their curriculum practices of locating themselves in areas where children played.

The next curriculum practice demonstrated by these educators was related to the type of emotional climate they created in their programs. This practice emerged as a dominant theme evidenced through the CLASS rating associated with the domain of Emotional Support (4.3). This rating indicated that participating educators created a moderately supportive emotional climate in their programs. Because this domain rating was based on a composite of four dimensions that reflected discrete curriculum practices assigned individual ratings ranging from 5.6 to 3.15, it is beneficial to discuss each dimension individually in order to gain a fuller understanding of the conceptual frameworks that inspire them.

Participating educators demonstrated strong practices in relation to creating an atmosphere that was free of sarcasm and punitive control of children. The strength behind these practices may be associated with their reported characteristics of caregiving, patience, and love of children that they described to be important in their work. This strength may also be associated with their demonstrated constructivist-inspired room arrangement practices. A number of experts who have written about early childhood curriculum urge educators to design classroom spaces that are well organized and that minimize children's frustrations by allowing easy access to equipment and materials (Curtis & Carter, 2008; Stacey, 2009). Perhaps the room arrangement practices demonstrated by these educators have served to create classroom spaces in which children feel they are in control, thereby minimizing disruptive behaviors that may require the use of punitive controls by educators.

These educators demonstrated average curriculum practices in association with positive climate and teacher sensitivity. They demonstrated inconsistency in participating in children's activities and in engaging in social conversations with children. In addition, they demonstrated average emotional connections with children as they sometimes responded to children's needs by acknowledging emotions and providing comfort, while at other times they were dismissive. These average ratings may be related to another practice these educators expressed: one of limited participation in children's play. The practices associated with dimensions of positive climate and teacher sensitivity are closely related to demonstrated practices of engaging with children's play. It may also be that practices associated with creating a positive climate and teacher sensitivity are practices more closely related to personality characteristics of educators than to practices learned through professional training.

The last dimension associated with creating an emotional climate in the program is regard for student perspective. This dimension was assigned the lowest average rating within the domain of emotional support. Participating educators demonstrated practices of sometimes following children's leads while at other times controlling children's initiatives by not responding to their ideas or restricting their physical movements. These practices may be associated with educators' conflicting views regarding children's capabilities. Study findings revealed that three educators reported a view of children as capable, while two educators reported a view of children as dependent on adults.

The next curriculum practice demonstrated by these educators was related to guiding children's learning. This practice was demonstrated in a number of ways as evidenced through the CLASS ratings of the cluster of practices associated with the domains of Classroom Organization Support and Instructional Support. The practices associated with the Classroom Organization Support domain captured the organizational flow of the classroom and indicated that all five educators demonstrated a reasonably organized classroom. Their practices demonstrated that the daily schedule followed the

135

rhythms of children's play and that they were prepared for activities carried out. However, they also demonstrated practices of having too many transitions in their programs that took too long, leaving children wandering around the classroom uncertain as to what was expected of them.

Within the domains of Emotional Support and Classroom Organization Support, the lowest rated practices demonstrated by these five educators were in association with guiding children's learning (behavior management; instructional learning formats). It may be that they felt more confident with their role of supporting children's emotional needs than with their role of guiding children's learning as they seldom engaged children in contributing ideas to resolve conflict situations and they rarely used effective questions, interesting materials, or hands-on opportunities. This difference in confidence may be associated with the recent shifts in child-care curriculum introduced in Ontario through the ELECT framework that requires educators to consider curriculum through a lens of play, development, and child-initiated practices. Four of these educators completed their professional training years ago (two educators 25 years ago; one educator 19 years ago; one educator 15 years ago). The constructivist-inspired ideas that emphasize concept development through play endorsed by this provincial framework echo current evidence informed practices that may be at odds with curriculum ideas that these educators learned through their professional training years earlier.

While the fifth educator was a more recent graduate (seven years ago) and while she did reference the ELECT document in our conversations, she also reported a belief that children were not capable in contributing to curriculum ideas. Through our conversation about influences of her curriculum decisions, this educator reported that she often deferred to using themes as her curriculum inspiration because the children had not demonstrated sufficient ideas that she could translate into curriculum activities. Having the belief that children are capable learners is essential to supporting learning through play (Chaille, 2008; Curtis & Carter, 2008). The reported absence of this belief in this educator may have influenced her practices related to fully maximizing children's play as a learning opportunity.

The lack of confidence among all five educators in guiding children's learning was highlighted by the low rating (2.15) assigned to curriculum practices through the CLASS Instructional Support domain. While they demonstrated the constructivist-inspired practice of locating themselves in areas where children were playing, once they reached those locations, they engaged in practices that were more reflective of an instructivist-inspired framework. As they moved around the classroom, educators connected with children through brief verbal interactions. They labelled children's actions, "Oh, you are playing hockey," or posed close-ended questions, "What color is that?" Educators demonstrated verbal interactions that did not invite sustained, rich discussions with children, causing these educators to easily move on to other locations. The demonstration of these short and uninspired verbal interactions may be described as missed opportunities in maximizing child-initiated play to facilitate co-construction of knowledge, deepen understandings of concepts, and strengthen concept integrations (Epstein, 2007).

Further analysis indicated that during the times when the educators were involved with children, all five demonstrated instructivist-inspired practices of transmitting facts to children and extracting correct answers about those facts from children. Their practices included planned activities that emphasized academic concepts of letter, number, color, and calendar recognition with few elaborations and explanations. They navigated through these activities by posing questions that required right/wrong answers ("What color are you using?"), or one-word responses that required the repeating of facts just provided ("Today is Monday. Who knows what day today is?"). Educators intensified their focus of academic concepts by engaging with children through verbal redirections that lead children to produce correct answers combined with verbal praise when children eventually offered the correct answer. Educators rarely queried children to explain their own thinking and seldom encouraged deeper thinking through the use of *why* and *how* questions.

These results are similar to results of other studies indicating consistently low ratings in the area of supporting children's learning when assessing program quality. A study investigating quality in pre-kindergarten programs in 11 states in the United States of America revealed low quality mean ratings of 2.20 for the Instructional Support domain subscale of the CLASS observation assessment (Howes, Burchinal, Pianta, Bryant, Early, Clifford, & Barbarin, 2008). A similar study conducted to investigate the relationship among program quality indicators and children's developmental outcomes revealed a low quality mean rating of 2.08 for the Instructional Support subscale of CLASS (Pianta et al., 2008). The results of these studies indicated that educators might require additional training in order to support children's learning.

The considerable emphasis on instructivist-inspired curriculum practices in guiding children's learning displayed by the educators of this study may be associated with several factors, including an uncertainty in fully understanding their roles in this process. This uncertainty may be reasonable given the conflicting messages found in early childhood education literature. Phrases such as *child-centered programs* dominate early childhood literature and curriculum textbooks offer advice such as *children should take the lead in curriculum.* This information may be contributing to educators' uncertainty as to how to guide children's learning without interfering with children's play. Much of early childhood literature has dichotomized child-centered and teacher-centered practices as either, promoting the former: this is a condition that has been described as having the capacity to paralyze educators when they interact with children (Curtis & Carter, 2008).

These educators' emphasis on instructivist-inspired practices in guiding children's learning may also be associated with an incomplete understanding of how to apply constructivist-inspired practices for that purpose. It may be that these educators have participated in professional training programs or professional development workshops that have not sufficiently supported their understanding of constructivist-inspired curriculum practices. Recent literature examining specialized training and professional development that focuses on strengthening educators' curriculum practices urges for an emphasis on how educators are being taught, not only on what they are being taught (Nimmo & Park, 2009; Wood & Bennett, 2000).

The last curriculum practice demonstrated by these educators was the practice of carrying out planned activities that were disconnected from direct observations of children's prior interests. This practice, consistent with those of an instructivist-inspired curriculum framework, emerged as a strong theme among four participating educators. Even though three educators posted forms in their classrooms for the purpose of collecting observations of children's interests as their source for future curriculum ideas, activities they carried out (a pre-packaged language program; an activity around a letter; a calendar activity; and a Christmas craft activity) were motivated by sources external to the interests of children. The demonstration of this practice may be pointing to a disconnection between these educators' skills and the complicated nature of translating observations of children's interests into curriculum. This requirement is one that is often taken for granted in early childhood education, but one that has been identified as complex, requiring greater attention in professional education (Baum & King, 2006; Wood & Bennett, 2000).

What are qualified early childhood educators' self-reported beliefs about curriculum?

The findings of this study reveal that the participating educators reported five beliefs about curriculum. All five beliefs are associated with a constructivist-inspired curriculum framework. Three of these beliefs emerged as strong themes among four educators (play is an important part of curriculum; recognition of children's ideas as essential to emergent curriculum; and observations of children's interests as the source for educator-planned activities), and two beliefs (children are capable; identified curriculum approach being followed as emergent) emerged as weak themes among three educators.

These three strong beliefs were reported among the same four participating educators. They described the virtues of play as an essential vehicle for engaging children in learning, the recognition of children's ideas as essential to emergent curriculum, and the importance of observations of children's interests as the source for educator-planned activities. They highlighted the value of play in helping children learn a number of concepts and the importance of being engaged with them during play in order to observe and record their ideas. These beliefs are consistent with principles of constructivist-inspired curriculum that promote play-based curriculum practices (Saracho & Spodek, 2002; Stacey, 2009). The reporting of these beliefs is consistent with findings from research studies investigating the beliefs of early childhood educators (Cassidy et al., 1995; McMullen & Alat, 2002).

These four educators may hold these strong beliefs because, as practicing educators in Ontario who had identified an awareness of the provincial curriculum framework ELECT, their focus of play and on observations of children's play as a source for curriculum may be heightened. The holding of these beliefs may also be associated with the professional development workshops they attended, as all four reported participating in curriculum-related workshops during the past year. These workshops may have emphasized the importance of recognizing children's ideas and recording observations of children's interests as the source for planned activities as essential to emergent curriculum.

One of the participating educators did not report any of these three beliefs as beliefs that she held. This educator explained that learning skills related to recognizing letters and numbers were an important part of her curriculum that she could more fully achieve through planned activities rather than through play. This educator graduated from a professional training program 25 years ago and may not have been exposed to these play-based practices through that training. While she did report that she had attended numerous workshops through her career, three within the last year, she may also hold strong personal beliefs about education and learning that had been developed over a long time and that may be difficult to change, as has been evidenced through research (Tillema, 1995).

The next belief revealed by three educators was that they were following an emergent curriculum approach in their programs. They described characteristics of emergent curriculum and related stories of how they implemented those characteristics in their daily practices. Educators' beliefs about the curriculum approach they were following may be associated with the professional development workshops they attended. These workshops may have included strong messages that emergent curriculum is the desired curriculum in Ontario and one that should be followed.

In addition to the belief they were following an emergent curriculum, the same three educators revealed the belief that children are capable learners. They exposed this view about children as they explained their commitment to emergent curriculum. Two educators reported the opposing view; that of children being dependent on adults. The same two educators described their approach to curriculum as being influenced more by themes than as being emergent. These reported beliefs revealed an interesting link between the view of children as capable and approach to curriculum. The view of children as being dependent on adults may be associated with the public perception of children as naïve, vulnerable beings in need of adult intervention for their learning (Dahlberg et al., 2007). The concept of adults leading children to reach their potential has been presented in a number of popular early childhood textbooks and has been examined through research (Langford, 2008). It may be that this view has been nurtured in these two educators through the literature they had been exposed to in their professional preparation.

How do qualified early childhood educators describe their professional identity?

The findings of this study reveal that participating educators described their professional identity through a lens of contradiction and professional vulnerability. They presented themselves as professionals who want to be valued by society for their specialized knowledge and expertise. However, their descriptions of their work were often inconsistent with those of professionals who have a strong understanding of and confidence in that specialized knowledge. Professional identity has been characterized as the result of interplay between what the professionals themselves perceive to be important about their work, and the influence and perceptions of other people about the value of their work (Tickle, 2000).

Through the presence of a strong emerging theme, four participating educators reported the belief that their work was misunderstood and undervalued by society. They declared a frustration in being viewed as babysitters who were not valued for their education and experience, a view that has been reported by other educators through research (Doherty et al., 2000; McGillivray, 2008). At the same time they described these frustrations, participating educators explained their work in a way that highlighted they might not fully value their own expertise. In describing qualities that make them effective educators, participants limited their answers to qualities such as being loving, patient, and caregiving. These are the same qualities that have been associated with a substitute mother (McGillivray, 2008; Moss, 2006) and might be associated with describing effective babysitters. Dominant social discourses that shape the public's view of educators have described educators as "having a good sense, being kind and loving, being warm and sensitive" (McGillivray, 2008, p. 250) rather than as professionals who have specialized credentials and expertise. These same discourses in North American society have contributed to a view of the educator as substitute mother associated with providing emotional support rather than cognitive stimulation to young children (Moss, 2006). It may be that during their working years through interactions with parents, family, friends, and the general public, these educators have experienced these socially dominant views about their work. It may therefore be that their own perceptions of their work have been influenced by these dominant social views.

Findings of this study also revealed that educators' commitment to the literature that shapes their profession and inspires their curriculum practices was vulnerable to the influences of others. This point emerged as a dominant theme as all five educators engaged in curriculum practices that were inconsistent with emergent curriculum, a curriculum approach that three educators reported to be using. Four participants described a focus on teaching letters to the children in their programs in association with praise from parents for teaching valuable skills rather than in association with observations of children's interests, a belief that the same four educators reported. One of these participants highlighted hand-over-hand teaching to satisfy a parent's request that her child learn to write her name and three of these participants demonstrated the use of documentation practices that focused more on making skills they were teaching visible to parents than on describing rich narratives of children's experiences as outlined by emergent curriculum.

Educators' longing to be valued by others for their work is a dominant theme in early childhood education professional identity literature (Doherty et al., 2000; Nimmo & Park, 2009). It may be that the educators in the current study also long to be valued by the parents of their programs for their work. Interestingly, they did not translate this longing into creating opportunities to educate parents about practices that they as professionals know are more suited to educating young children. Rather, they deferred to implementing practices that parents requested or that parents may have easily recognized as being educational. Educational practices associated with constructivist-inspired curriculum in early childhood education are not easily recognized by the general public and have been dismissed by many as being just play (Katz, 1999). In order for these educators to convince others of the value of the practices they know as professionals they should be engaging in to guide children's

143

learning, they may require a deeper understanding of how those practises relate to the development of skills such as letter and number recognition, skills that are more easily recognized by the general public. These educators may not have a strong enough understanding of the literature and research associated with their professional practices in order to explain and defend them fully to parents. This condition may have made them vulnerable to the influences of others' suggestions about how to guide children's learning.

In addition, all five educators displayed a lack of confidence in their own professional knowledge by implementing practices based on advice from others who were not directly engaged with the children in their programs and who would not have had the same level of knowledge about those children as they did. Participating educators described using fill-in-the-blanks documentation forms and generic conflict resolution strategies proposed to them by workshop leaders and external consultants, as well as off-the-shelf language programs recommended to them by elementary teachers. They described using these practices without evidence of modifying them to correspond with distinctive characteristics of their own programs or to the children within their programs.

Early childhood literature and research associated with emergent curriculum describes curriculum practices as complex strategies that are inspired through professional decision-making within the context of observations of children's development and interests, not as simple techniques that can easily be repeated from one situation to another (Curtis & Carter, 2008; Stacey, 2009). These educators may not have a strong enough understanding of emergent curriculum practices in order to exercise professional decision-making to generate their own solutions to problems they encountered through their programs. They may also hold a stronger value for the knowledge of other professionals than their own knowledge. This condition may have influenced their decisions to implement recommendations provided by others without questioning them. This may be especially true in relation to elementary teachers'

144

knowledge as two educators stated that the language programs recommended must be beneficial because they were being used in schools.

What are the relations among educational and professional backgrounds of qualified early childhood educators and their self-reported beliefs about curriculum, their practices of curriculum, and their descriptions of professional identity?

The findings of this study revealed that participating educators shared a number of educational and professional characteristics. All five educators obtained the required credential to work in a licensed child-care center from a college Early Childhood Education program, and all five attended a local community college. Four of these five educators enrolled in their college programs right after high school. One educator had a degree from another country and found employment in a licensed child care center while she returned to complete her diploma program through an apprenticeship route.

All five participating educators worked in a licensed child-care center with preschool aged children (three to five years) at the time of the study. One educator had worked in the field under 10 years (seven years); two educators under 20 years (19 and 15 years) and two educators over 20 years (25 and 24 years). Three of these educators had worked in the same child-care center during their entire employment as educators; one had worked in two different child-care centers and one in three different child-care centers.

The findings of this study revealed very few relationships among educators' professional and educational backgrounds and their beliefs about curriculum, practices of curriculum, and professional identity. All participating educators demonstrated constructivist-inspired practices in relation to their classroom arrangement and presence of posted descriptions of their curriculum plans, also both practices that are

145

associated with licensing requirements. While the format of their posted descriptions of curriculum plans differed as some included a listing of activities while others described these plans within a context of children's observations and connections to other classroom experiences, these differences did not appear to be related to educational or professional backgrounds. In addition, all participants demonstrated largely instructivist-inspired practices in guiding children's learning regardless of educational and professional backgrounds.

Study findings did reveal a difference in relation to the practice of posted documentations and educational background. The educator who graduated most recently (2009) posted documentations that included pictures of children's experiences in combination with a written description of those experiences. She posted these documentations at child height inviting children to revisit the experiences, as inspired by a constructivist framework. This difference may be attributed to her fuller understanding of this practice that she may have learned through her more recent professional training.

In the areas of beliefs about curriculum and professional identity, study findings did not reveal any patterns that may have been related to educational and professional backgrounds. The absence of strong patterns in these areas intimates that considerations other than professional and educational backgrounds of these educators may need to be explored.

What are the relationships among beliefs about curriculum, curriculum practices, and professional identities in qualified early childhood educators?

The findings of this study disclosed a number of complex relationships among beliefs about curriculum, curriculum practices, and professional identities of participating educators. These relationships reveal that educators' professional identity may have acted as a more persuasive guide to curriculum practices than educators'

146

beliefs about curriculum. These relationships further reveal that in forming their professional identity, educators presented a portrait of professionals whose confidence in the literature and research that shapes their profession may be vulnerable to the influences of others (e.g., parents, teachers, others in society). These relationships are represented through the model in Figure 8.

Constructivist-inspired..**Instructivist-inspired**

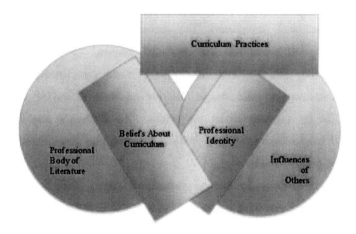

Figure 8. Relationships among beliefs about curriculum, curriculum practices, and professional identity

All five educators participating in this study had obtained their diplomas in Early Childhood Education through professional training programs, and all five worked in licensed child-care settings in Ontario. These educators are members of a profession that is shaped by its own unique body of knowledge (Bennett, 2005; Bredekamp & Copple, 1997; DeVries & Kohlberg, 1990) and is endorsed through the provincial curriculum framework. This body of knowledge and the practices it inspires differ from the body of knowledge that has shaped traditional practices in education

(DeVries & Kohlberg, 1999). Traditional practices have been described as being influenced by principles that place a greater value on didactic learning and academically oriented facts, and have been associated with the use of instructivist practices as a method of achieving the acquisition of those facts (DeVries & Kohlberg, 1999; Marlowe & Page, 1998). Traditional practices have been associated more with elementary and secondary education than with early childhood education.

Through their reported beliefs, four participating educators of this study demonstrated a connection with the body of knowledge that shapes their profession. They revealed a number of strong beliefs that characterize constructivist-inspired curriculum practices (the value of play as an essential component of curriculum; the recognition of children's ideas as essential to curriculum; and observations of children's interests as the source for planned activities) that are endorsed by their profession. In addition, three of these educators distinguished their approach to curriculum as emergent. However, a closer examination of demonstrated practices revealed a disconnection between reported beliefs about curriculum and practices among these four educators.

The disconnect between educators' beliefs about curriculum and curriculum practices has been documented through early childhood education research (File & Gullo, 2002; Kagan, 1992; Maxwell et al., 2001; Vartuli, 1999; Wilcox-Herzog, 2002). Those study findings indicated that professional training does not consistently translate into constructivist-inspired practices (File & Gullo, 2002; Vartuli, 1999). Authors of those studies highlighted educators' capacities to hold opposing beliefs about curriculum and identified this condition as contributing to the presence of curriculum practices that contradicts beliefs about curriculum (Green, 1971). In addition, their findings suggest that educators' incomplete understanding of a constructivist framework might be associated with their implementation of practices that oppose their beliefs (Maxwell et al., 2001; Wilcox-Herzog, 2002).

148

The findings of the current study revealed that participating educators did not report opposing beliefs about curriculum as all four of the same educators conveyed constructivist-inspired beliefs (emphasizing play to be important part of curriculum; identifying children's interests as essential to curriculum; identifying observations of children's interests as a source for planned activities; a view of children as capable; and describing their approach to curriculum as emergent). However, similar to findings of other studies, their demonstrated practices of guiding children's learning were inconsistent with these conveyed beliefs as they engaged in practices that appeared to be inspired more by an instructivist framework. This condition was evidenced through their low ratings (2.33; 2.17; 1.67; 2.74; and 1.84) associated with the Instructional Support Domain of the CLASS Observation Assessment. They transmitted facts to children through drill and practice and used praise and redirection to motivate and reinforce desired behavior in children. Their interactions with children were largely free of meaningful conversations that integrated children's thinking or engaged children in uncovering deeper understandings of concepts. In addition, they implemented planned activities that were disconnected from children's interests.

In addition to these findings, study results revealed an interesting pattern linking the belief of children as capable and educators' identification of their approach to curriculum as emergent, as the two educators who reported the belief that children were not capable were the same two educators who described their approach to curriculum as being theme-based. This link has been described by authors who have written about curriculum as being a necessary condition for the implementation of constructivist-inspired practices (Chaille, 2008; Dietze & Kashin, 2012; Jacobs et al., 2007).

The strength of the disconnect between educators' constructivist-inspired reported beliefs about curriculum and their demonstrated instructivist-inspired practices of supporting children's learning draws attention to two influencing factors: professional identity of educators and educators understanding of a constructivist-

149

inspired curriculum framework. In considering professional identity, this disconnect highlights the influence of others on educators' confidence in their practices.

Professional identity has been characterized as the interplay between what the professionals themselves perceive to be important in their work and the influence and perceptions of other people about the value of that work (Tickle, 2000). The ways in which early childhood educators view themselves appear to be intricately connected with the ways in which others view them. Study findings have revealed that others view the work of educators as "mindless, custodial work," and refer to those engaged in that work as babysitters (Nimmo & Park, 2009; Kagan & Cohen, 1997). Findings also indicate that even when educators express confidence in their professional knowledge and skills, they report that their capabilities and contributions are not recognized by the general public (Doherty et al., 2000; Kagan & Cohen, 1997), by family, friends, or the parents of the children within their programs (Whitebrook & Sakai, 2004).

Four of the educators who participated in this study reported being referred to as babysitters by others and reported feeling frustrated with this label. It has been proposed through early childhood education literature that society's view of educators as low-skilled babysitters has made them vulnerable to engaging in practices for the specified purpose of elevating others' views of the value of their work (Nimmo & Park, 2009).

Findings of the current study revealed a link between educators' reported view of being misunderstood and undervalued by society and their engaging in practices in order to increase being valued by parents for teaching important skills to children. These two conditions were associated with the same four educators as all four reported that they were misunderstood and undervalued by society and all four demonstrated instructivist-inspired practices of teaching letters to children in association with praise from parents. It may be that their practices of guiding children's learning may have been influenced by a desire to be viewed by parents as teaching children valuable skills.

In addition, four educators implemented the constructivist-inspired practice of documentation; however, the demonstration of this practice by three of these educators appeared to be more associated with making the value of their work visible to parents rather than with the constructivist-inspired purpose of making children's learning visible to the classroom community.

These educators' practices also disclosed a surrendering of curriculum decisions to others. All five educators reported deferring to the advice of others they identified as experts to direct their curriculum practices without question. These experts (workshop leaders; consultants from external agencies; and elementary teachers) did not appear to have been directly involved with the children in the programs and would not have had the same level of knowledge of the children's development or interests that these educators had. However, these educators reported that they followed their advice with no evidence of questioning or modifying the recommendations provided.

Through this surrendering of curriculum decisions to others, these educators revealed a devaluing of their professional education and of self as a knowledgeable contributor to children's learning. They revealed a stronger value for the professional knowledge of others than their own, a value that two educators emphasized in relation to elementary school teachers. Through these practices, educators presented a view of themselves as passive consumers of other experts' knowledge, a view that may be especially problematic if they are to engage in constructivist-inspired practices that require them to embrace action research and reflective thinking in order to generate contextually specific practices.

These educators demonstrated a lack confidence in their abilities to generate curriculum practices within a context of observations of children's development and interests as inspired by the literature and research that shapes their profession. This lack of confidence was also evident as educators engaged in instructivist-inspired practices to achieve child outcomes that were requested by parents or more easily recognized by parents as traditional child learnings (writing their name; recognizing colors; reciting days of the week; memorizing numbers), rather than describing to parents the benefits of constructivist-inspired practices that are more suitable to guiding children's learning and that are endorsed by their profession.

For these educators to confidently implement curriculum practices inspired by their professional knowledge and reported beliefs without being swayed by the influences of others, they may require the formation of a professional identity that is resilient to society's views of their profession. Achieving this may not be an easy task as the formation of these educators' professional identity may also be complicated by the influence of personal beliefs they have developed over time through their own experiences as learners (Kagan, 1992; Pajares, 1992). As members of society, these educators may have participated as learners in educational experiences that were undoubtedly influenced by instructivist-inspired practices. These educational experiences may have contributed to shaping their views about education, about teaching and learning, and their image of educators.

All of the educators participating in the current study surrounded themselves with traditional images of education. Their classrooms contained a number of symbols (cut out letters; color charts; cut out numbers; and calendars) associated with more traditional instructivist-inspired practices. They all carried out curriculum activities in which they instructed children to reproduce letters, identify colors, or memorize days of the week. These practices may be associated with their own socially constructed beliefs of education that they may have developed over a long period of time through instructivist-inspired learning experiences. As a result, these beliefs may be strong and deeply entrenched and therefore difficult to change (Nisbett & Ross, 1980; Tillema, 1995). Other study findings examining views of educational practices have revealed that educators' long-standing personal beliefs act as a filter to newly accumulated professional knowledge (Kagan, 1992). They also indicate that educators' personal

152

beliefs are not easily swayed by newly encountered knowledge, even if that knowledge includes significant evidence and confirmation by their profession (Kagan, 1992; Pajares, 1992; Richardson, 2003).

Early childhood literature describes constructivist practices as complex strategies inspired through professional decision-making within the context of observations of children's development and interests, not as simple techniques that can easily be repeated from one situation to another (Curtis & Carter, 2008; Stacey, 2009). Educators participating in this study revealed an incomplete understanding of a constructivist framework as all five demonstrated instructivist-inspired practices in association with guiding children's learning during free-play and during planned activities. All five participating educators had graduated with professional training from early childhood education programs. In addition, all five participating educators engaged in professional development for the purpose of enhancing their understanding of curriculum and reported that this engagement was useful to their curriculum practices.

Empowering educators to develop confidence in their practices through a strong understanding of a constructivist framework may require a reconceptualization of professional training. Professional training has traditionally focused on teaching practices to educators with little attention paid to examining educational theories and principles that inspire them (Tatto, 1998) and even less attention paid to integrating these practices with educators' beliefs and attitudes (Baum & King, 2006). This omission has been described as problematic in supporting educators to fully understand and embrace constructivist-inspired practices (Tatto, 1998). This omission may also nurture a perception among educators that curriculum practices are techniques to be learned and may contribute to a view of self as technician who applies these techniques. This perception has been described as contributing to the formation of a professional identity where educators see themselves as consumers of

153

others' expertise rather than as constructors of their own expertise and professional decision makers (Moss, 2006).

Through their reported beliefs, educators participating in this study described a strong commitment to the professional body of literature that shapes their profession. They revealed a desire to contribute to children's learning and to be valued for that contribution. At the same time, they demonstrated uncertainty in their practices and a professional identity that appeared to be vulnerable to the influences of others. In order to resist these influences, these educators may require professional education opportunities that empower them through a process of value examination and theory construction toward a view of self as reflective and capable professional.

Chapter 6: Conclusion

In this chapter I present the conclusions of this study. I begin this section by describing those conclusions. Next I present the implications of study results for educators and for the professional education (pre-service and professional development) of those educators. Then I present the limitations of this study and conclude by offering suggestions for future research.

The purpose of this study was to examine the inter-relationships among curriculum practices, beliefs about curriculum and professional identity. Study findings have exposed the presence of a number of emerging themes that have provided an explanation of the relationships among curriculum practices, beliefs about curriculum and professional identity. While these findings have not produced definitive conclusions or causal associations among curriculum practices, beliefs about curriculum and professional identity, the themes that have emerged and the relationships among those themes have uncovered some implications for early childhood educators and for the professional education of those educators.

First and foremost, this study reinforces that the implementation of curriculum practices in early childhood education is a complex process that is not achieved simply or easily through professional training. Findings have revealed a complicated interplay between educators' beliefs about curriculum and professional identity in influencing their curriculum practices and specifically highlight educators' confidence in understanding and owning their professional literature, and the influences of others in that interplay.

Study Conclusions

Educators of this study revealed a strong desire to contribute to children's learning and to be valued for that contribution. They all completed professional education

155

programs specializing in early childhood education, and participated in on-going professional development while they worked for the specified purpose of enhancing their knowledge of current curriculum practices. These educators articulated strong constructivist inspired beliefs about curriculum that reflect the literature that shapes their profession. However, their demonstrated practices exposed a disconnection from those beliefs.

Four of these educators reported constructivist-inspired beliefs as they described the importance of play in curriculum, the recognizing of children's ideas in how curriculum evolves and the observing of children's interests as the source of their planned activities. However, these educators did not translate their beliefs fully and completely into practice. While all four located themselves in the areas where children played, they did not fully engage with children through play. While three of these educators posted forms for the purpose of gathering observations of children's interests, they did not complete those observations or use them as a source for their planned activities. The findings of this study have proposed the following influences to that disconnect: incomplete understanding of professional literature; influences of parents and public perception; vulnerable professional identity; and personal beliefs about children, learning and education.

In addition, all five educators of this study consistently demonstrated instructivist-inspired practices in supporting children's learning. These practices conflicted with early childhood education literature and research, and contradicted their reported beliefs about curriculum. They revealed a lack of understanding in how to engage with children through meaningful interactions that uncovered deeper understandings of concepts and integrated children's thinking.

Participating educators demonstrated an incomplete understanding of a constructivist framework and the practices it inspires. Four educators created documentations of children's learning and posted those documentations in their classrooms. However, the format of those documentations and the locations of where they were posted revealed a limited understanding of the purpose of documentation as inspired by a constructivist framework. This resulted in educators' not fully maximizing documentation as a strategy that invites children to revisit experiences for the purpose of uncovering deeper meanings and contributing to the emergence of future curriculum directions. This may also have contributed to focusing educators to implement this practice as a communication tool for the value of their work to parents.

The curriculum practices of participating educators appeared to be easily swayed by the influences of others. These practices revealed a professional identity that did not appear to be fully inspired by their beliefs about curriculum or their professional literature. All five participating educators engaged in practices that were inspired by an authority from other people without questioning or modifying. These included fill-in-the-blanks documentation forms, generic conflict resolution strategies and off-the-shelf curriculum programs. In addition, four educators described teaching letters to the children in the programs in association with praise or request by parents. A number of these practices (generic conflict resolution strategies and-the-shelf curriculum programs) and the ways in which they were carried out by these educators (disconnected from observations of children's interests) were instructivist-inspired practices that contradicted educators' own reported beliefs about curriculum and their professional literature.

Based on these study findings, I offer the following implications for educators with a view to strengthening their confidence in the implementation of curriculum practices that are more aligned with their own professional knowledge and beliefs about curriculum. Furthermore, in recognition that educators require support in the development of this confidence, I offer additional implications for those involved in the delivery of professional education of those educators.

Implications for early childhood educators

Educators would benefit from an enhanced understanding of the theories and principles that define a constructivist framework within a context of how children develop and how they learn. This would enable educators to engage in curriculum practices that complement the characteristics of the children they are working with and the contexts of their programs and would serve to translate their knowledge and beliefs about curriculum more fully and completely into practice.

This enhanced understanding may assist educators to gain greater thought and confidence in their skills and abilities and may empower them to hold on to their already reported constructivist-inspired beliefs about curriculum (the importance of play in curriculum; the recognizing of children's ideas in how curriculum evolves; and the observing of children's interests as the source of their planned activities). Through a fuller understanding of a constructivist framework educators may gain confidence in generating practices that allow them to translate their beliefs into practice, enhance their abilities to guide children's learning, exercise their professional knowledge, and elevate their view of self as reflective educator.

This newly found confidence may contribute to a shift in educators' view of self as knowledgeable, capable professional and may empower educators to describe their curriculum practices to parents with assurance, resist the reducing of their professional decision making into simple techniques that can be carried out through pre-packaged programs and fill-in-the-blanks forms, and challenge the socially constructed view of educators as babysitters.

In addition, educators would benefit to engage in an examination of their personal beliefs about children, learning, and education. Research studies have described educators' personal beliefs as a filter to their professional knowledge (Kagan, 1992), and an influence on their curriculum practices (File & Gullo, 2002). The examination of personal beliefs would provide educators with the opportunity to make their beliefs visible. Through this process they may become more self-aware about how their

158

personal beliefs might interface with their professional beliefs and practices. This recognition may contribute to a greater awareness and understanding about the possible disconnection between beliefs and practices and may empower educators to become vigilant in attending to it.

Finally, educators would benefit to become more comfortable with uncertainty. Constructivist inspired practices require educators to embrace possibilities and uncertainties, as the directions of curriculum will not be in their control alone and might not always be clear. These practices invite educators and children to engage in a collaborative process of meaning making that is filled with possibility, opportunity, and risk-taking. Through this process of co-construction, educators support children to integrate learning, build theories, and learn facts. Becoming comfortable with uncertainty may be a risky proposition for educators as it may challenge the socially constructed image they have of self as educator: someone who should always be in control and someone who should know all the answers. All participants of this study revealed glimpses of what may have been their socially constructed image of an educator as they demonstrated practices of focusing on right/wrong answers, managing the classroom environment and carrying out predictable, single focused activities.

Implications for the professional education of educators

Those involved in the professional education of others, both at the pre-service and on-going professional learning levels should resist teaching curriculum to students/educators as techniques that reduce practices to formulaic sequences and undermine children's and educators' contributions. In addition, they should resist teaching curriculum without engaging in a deep examination of the principles that inspire practices, the historical and socio-political values that influence practices and the personal beliefs that interface with their implementation. Those involved in this process should create opportunities for students and educators to investigate learning theories

159

and principles at a deeper level, to examine ideas and concepts meaningfully and from various perspectives, and to question, challenge and develop an inquiry based approach to their own learning. They should nurture the development of co-learning, on-going learning and re-learning that highlight reflection, introspection and a profound consideration how societal values and personal beliefs influence curriculum practices.

These features to professional education may contribute to a fuller, more complete understanding of the complexity of curriculum, an understanding that may empower educators to re-position their relationship with traditional images of learning and teaching, and inspire more suitable learning opportunities for the children in their programs. This more complete understanding may also strengthen educators' confidence in the soundness of their practices and may empower them to translate their reported constructivist-inspired beliefs about curriculum without being influenced by the misplaced suggestions of others. Finally, this more complete understanding may inspire a view of the self in educators as more knowledgeable professionals and may contribute to the formation of a stronger professional identity that may inspire educators to see themselves as action researchers who generate knowledge, rather than as technicians who use other people's knowledge (Moss, 2006).

These approaches to professional education may be of particular importance to those who are engaged in the creation and delivery of on-going professional learning of educators who have been working in the field for a considerable period of time. These educators may require a transitioning from one set of practices that may be influenced by more instructivist principles into a new set of practices that are more constructivist-inspired and reflective of current literature and research. As these educators may have a repertoire of practices they have developed through their working years with children, they may require a deconstruction and reconstruction of their curriculum practices, a process that may not be possible through simply learning new strategies and techniques (Baum & King, 2006; Tatto, 1998). This condition was evidenced by the educators who participated in this study as all reported to have participated in curriculum workshops

160

that familiarized them with the provincial curriculum framework ELECT and emergent curriculum. However, the demonstrated practices of these educators were not consistent with either ELECT or emergent curriculum practices.

Those involved in the delivery of professional education, both at the pre-service and on-going professional learning levels should also examine resources (textbooks, articles, etc.) they present to students/educators for the messages they may portray about children's capabilities and contributions to learning, about educators roles in supporting children's learning, and about the value of educators' work. Images of children sitting in groups while educators deliver facts to them as depicted through books and classroom posters may contribute to educators' perceptions of their role as instructor of knowledge and children's role as recipient of that knowledge. Images of number and color charts, alphabet letters, shapes and days of the week as depicted by classroom posters may contribute to educators' perception of the essentials for curriculum. Statements that emphasize educator's work as *caregiving, nurturing and loving* as depicted through textbooks may guide educators' perceptions of the primary focus to their work. These images through resources have the capacity to influence the formation of educators' perceptions about their roles in subtle yet powerful ways (Langford, 2008).

Limitations of the Study

While this study was carried out with particular attention to trustworthiness and credibility, there are some limitations that are worthy of mention. The first of these is that the study involved five female educators who worked full-time with preschool aged children in five different licensed child-care centres located in one province generalizing the results of this study should be done with caution. However, as some of the characteristics of these participating educators are dominant characteristics of the child-care workforce (female; college diploma as the highest credential obtained) these findings may be transferable to some degree.

The second limitation of the study is that while the participating educators all had a college diploma, they all reported that they had attended their local college. As this study took place in one geographical location that has only one college offering this credential, all participants were graduates of the same college. The third limitation of the study is the lack of full and complete member checking of all data collected. While member checking of curriculum practices did occur as I initiated conversations with each participant by recalling specific observations that were gathered through the CLASS observation assessment, I did not employ the same rigor in relation to verifying each participant's responses to beliefs about curriculum and descriptions of professional identity.

The final limitation of the study may be influence of the researcher. While I paid considerable attention to being respectful and non-judgmental as I engaged participants in conversation about their beliefs and practices, I cannot ignore that the mere fact that I was asking questions about these topics may have been an influence on participants' responses. The responses of these participants may have been influenced by a professional desirability as they may have provided answers they through I wished to hear.

Suggestions for Further Research

This study could be replicated in other geographical locations where educators might have attended different college programs, and with educators who have greater diversity in years at which they graduated (new graduates, educators who graduated ten years ago, educators who graduated twenty years ago) to investigate the influence of different post-secondary early childhood education programs and different years of graduation on educator beliefs about curriculum, curriculum practices and professional identity. The study could also be replicated with educators who work with other age groups (infants, toddlers, school age children) to examine if the age of the children that educators work with is related to these constructs and their inter-relationships.

In addition, the role of how other colleagues' practices and beliefs about curriculum influence educators' practices, beliefs and professional identity should also be investigated. These influences have been examined through other research studies in relation to curriculum practices (Nelson, 2000), but have not been extended to the influence of supervisors and fellow colleagues on the educators' beliefs about curriculum or professional identity.

Finally, as educators usually work as part of a team in child-care centers, the formation of professional identity within a context of child-care centre culture and child-care center systems should also be examined. These examinations would provide valuable findings and may reveal a strengthened understanding of professional identity of educators.

References

Anderson, L. (2001). Nine prospective teachers and their experiences in teacher education: The role of entering conceptions of teaching and learning. In B. Torff & R.J. Sternberg (Eds.). *Understanding and teaching the intuitive mind: Student and teacher learning.* Mahwash, NJ: Erlbaum.

Arnett, J. (1989). Caregivers in day-care centers: Does training matter? *Journal of Applied Developmental Psychology, 10,* 541-552. doi:10.1016/0193-3973(89)90026-9.

Asher, S., Singleton, L., Tinsley, B., & Hymel, S. (1979). Peer relation rating scale. *Developmental Psychology, 15,* 443-444.

Baum, A., & King, M. (2006). Creating a climate of self-awareness in early childhood teacher preparation programs. *Early Childhood Education Journal, 33,* 217-222.

Beach, J., Bertrand, J., Forer, B., Michal. D., & Tougas, J. (2004). *Working for change: Canada's child care workforce.* Retrieved from http://www.ccsc-cssge.ca/sites/default/files/uploads/About%20CCHRSC%20Docs/WorkingforChangeMain_Eng.pdf

Beach, J., Friendly M., Ferns, C., Prabhu, N., & Forer, B. (2009). *Early childhood education and care in Canada 2008.* Toronto, Canada: Childcare Research and Resource Unit.

Beijaard, D., Meijer, P., & Verloop, N. (2004). Reconsidering research on teachers' professional identity. *Teaching and Teacher Education, 20,* 107-128.

Beijaard, D., Verloop, N., & Vermunt, J. (2000). Teachers' perceptions of professional identity: An exploratory study from a person knowledge perspective. *Teaching and Teacher Education, 16,* 749-764.

Bennett, J. (2005). Curriculum issues in national policy-making. *European Early Childhood Education Research Journal, 13,* 5-23.

Black, A., & Ammon P. (1992). A developmental-constructivist approach to teacher education. *Journal of Teacher Education, 43,* 323-335.

Booth, C. (1997). The fiber project: One teacher's adventure toward emergent curriculum. *Young Children, 52,* 79-85.

Boudourides, M. (2003). Constructivism, education, science and technology. *Canadian Journal of Learning and Technology, 29,* 5-20.

Bredekamp, S., & Copple, S. (Eds.). (1997). *Developmentally appropriate practices in early childhood programs.* Washington, DC: National Association for the Education of Young Children.

Britzman, D. P. (1992). The terrible problem of knowing thyself: Toward a post-structural account of teacher identity. *Journal of Curriculum Theorizing, 9,* 23-46.

Brooks, M., & Brooks, J. (1999). The courage to be constructivist. *Educational Leadership, 57,* 18-24.

Brooks, M., & Brooks-Grennon, J. (1999) *In search of understanding: The case for constructivist classrooms.* Alexandria, VA: Association for Supervision and Curriculum Development.

Bryant, D. M., Clifford, R. M., & Peisner, E. S. (1991). Best practices for beginners: Developmental appropriateness in kindergarten. *American Educational Research Journal, 28,* 783-803.

Burchinal, R. M., Cryer, D., Clifford, R. M., & Howes C. (2002). Caregiver training and classroom quality in child care centers. *Applied Developmental Science, 6,* 2-11.

Burchinal, R. M., Peisner-Feinber, E., Bryant, D. M., & Clifford, R. (2000). Children's social and cognitive development and child care quality: Testing for differential associations related to poverty, gender, or ethnicity. *Applied Developmental Science, 4,* 149-165.

Burts, D. C., Hart, C., Charlesworth, R., & Kirk, L. (1990). A comparison of stress behaviors in kindergarten children in classrooms with developmentally appropriate versus developmentally inappropriate instructional practices. *Early Childhood Research Quarterly, 5,* 407-423.

Cassidy, D. J., Buell, M. J., Pugh-Hoese, S., & Russell, P. (1995). The effect of education on child care teachers' beliefs and classroom quality: Year one evaluation of the TEACH early childhood associate degree scholarship program. *Early Childhood Research Quarterly, 10,* 171-183.

Cassidy, D. J., & Lawrence, J. M. (2000). Teachers' beliefs: The "whys" behind the "how tos" in child care classrooms. *Journal of Research in Childhood Education, 14,* 193-204.

Chaille, C. (2008). *Constructivism across the curriculum in early childhood classrooms: Big ideas as inspiration.* New York: Pearson Publishing.

Charlesworth, R., Hart, C., Burts, D., Thomasson, R., Mosley, J., & Fleege, P. (1993). Measuring the developmental appropriateness of kindergarten teachers' beliefs and practices. *Early Childhood Research Quarterly, 8,* 255-276.

Clifford, P. G. (1992). The myth of empowerment. *Nursing Administrator, 163,* 1-5.

Coffey, A., & Atkinson, P. (1996). *Making sense of qualitative data analysis: Complementary strategies.* Thousand Oaks, CA: Sage.

Crawford, P., Brown, B., & Majomi, P. (2008). Professional identity in community mental health nursing: A thematic analysis. *International Journal of Nursing Studies, 45,* 1055-1063.

Creswell, J. W. (2007). *Qualitative inquiry and research design: Choosing among five approaches.* Thousand Oaks, CA: Sage.

Crowther, I. (2003). *Creating effective learning environments.* Scarborough, ON: Nelson Thompson Learning.

Curtis, D., & Carter, M. (2008). *Learning together with young children: A curriculum framework for reflective teachers.* St. Paul, MN: Redleaf Press.

Dahlberg, G., Moss, P., & Pence, A. (2007). *Beyond quality in early childhood education and care: Languages of evaluation* (2nd ed.). New York, NY: Routledge.

Dall'Alba, G. (1991). The role of teaching in higher education: Enabling students to enter a field of study and practice. *Learning and Instruction. 3,* 299-313.

Day, C. A., Kington, G., Stobard, L., & Sammons, P. (2006). The personal and professional selves of teachers: Stable and unstable identities. *British Educational Research Journal, 32,* 601-616.

Day Nurseries Act. R.S.O. (1990). Ministry of Child and Youth Services, Ontario: Queen's Printer.

DeVries. R., Haney, J. P., & Zan, B. (1991). Sociomoral atmosphere in direct-instruction, eclectic, and constructivist kindergartens: A study of teachers' enacted interpersonal understanding. *Early Childhood Research Quarterly, 6,* 449-471.

DeVries, R., & Kohlberg, L. (1990). *Constructivist early education: Overview and comparison with other programs.* Washington, DC: National Association for the Education of Young Children.

DeVries, R., Reese-Learned, H., & Morgan, P. (1991). Sociomoral development in direct-instruction, eclectic, and constructivist-kindergartens: A study of children's enacted interpersonal understanding. *Early Childhood Research Quarterly, 6,* 473-517.

Dietze, B., & Kashin, D. (2012). *Playing and learning in early childhood education.* Toronto, ON: Pearson.

Dodge, D. (1988). *The creative curriculum for early childhood.* Washington, DC: Teaching Strategies.

Dodge, D. (1995). The importance of curriculum in achieving quality child day care programs. *Child Welfare, 74,* 1171-1188.

Doherty, G., & Forer, B. (2005). *Shedding new light on staff recruitment and retention challenges in child care.* Retrieved from Child Care Human Resources Sector

Council website: http://www.cccc-cssge.ca/sites/default/files/uploads/Projects-Pubs-Docs/2.33-SheddingLight_Eng.pdf

Doherty, G., Lero, D. S., Goelman, H., La Grange, A., & Tougas, J. (2000). *You bet I care! A Canada wide study on wages, working conditions and practices in child care centers.* Guelph, ON: Center for Families, Work and Wellbeing, University of Guelph.

Doolittle, P. E., & Camp, W. G. (1999). Constructivism: The career and technical education perspective. *Journal of Vocational and Technical Education. 16,* 23-46.

Duckworth, E. (1987). *The having of wonderful ideas and other essays on teaching and learning.* New York, NY: Teachers College Press.

Edwards, S. (2003). New directions: Charting the paths for the role of sociocultural theory in early childhood education and curriculum. *Contemporary Issues in Early Childhood, 4,* 251-266.

Eisenhardt, K. (1989). Building theories from case study research. *Academy of Management Review. 14, 523-550.*

Epstein, A. (2007). *The intentional teacher: Choosing the best strategies for young children's learning.* Washington, DC: National Association for the Education of Young Children.

Fairclough, N. (2003). *Analyzing discourse: Textual analysis for social research.* New York, NY: Routledge.

Fealy, G. M. (2004). The good nurse: Visions and values in images of the nurse. *Journal of Advanced Nursing, 46,* 649-656.

Fenech, M., & Sumsion, J. (2007). Early childhood teachers and regulation: Complicating power relations using a Foucauldian lens. *Contemporary Issues in Early Childhood, 8,* 109-122.

File, N. (1994). Children's play, teacher-child interactions, and teacher beliefs in integrated early childhood programs. *Early Childhood Quarterly, 9* (2), 223-240.

File, N., & Gullo, D. (2002). A comparison of early childhood and elementary education students' beliefs about primary classroom teaching practices. *Early Childhood Research Quarterly, 17,* 126-137.

Flyvbjerg, B. (2006). Five misunderstandings about case-study research. *Qualitative Inquiry, 12,* 219-245.

Foucault, M. (1980). *Power/knowledge: Selected interviews and other writings 1972-1977.* C. Gordon (Ed.). New York, NY: Pantheon Books.

Friendly, M., Doherty, G., & Beach, J. (2006). *Quality by design: What do we know about quality in early learning and child care, and what do we think? A literature review.* Toronto, ON; Childcare Research and Resource Unit, University of Toronto.

Gardner, D. M. (1942). *Testing results in the infant school.* London: Methuen.

Goffin, S. G. (1994). *Curriculum models and early childhood education, appraising the relationship.* New York, NY: Macmillan.

Goodson, I. F., & Cole, A. L. (1994). Exploring the teachers professional knowledge: Constructing identity and community. *Teacher Education Quarterly, 21,* 85-105.

Green, T. (1971). *The activities of teaching.* New York, NY: McGraw-Hill.

Guest, Bunce, & Johnson. (2006). How many interviews are enough? An experiment with data saturation and variability. *Field Research, 18,* 59-82.

Hamre, B., Mashburn, A., Pianta, R., & Downer, J. (2006). Validation of 3-factor model for classroom quality across preschool to fifth grade. *Early Childhood Research Quarterly, 15*(2), 167-184.

Harms, T., Clifford, R. M., & Cryer, D. (1998). *Early Childhood Environment Rating Scale: Revised Edition.* New York: Teachers College Press.

Hart, C., Burts, D., Charlesworth, R., Fleege, P., Ickes, M., & Durland, M. (1990). Instructional activities and teacher beliefs scale.

Hart, C., Burts, D., & Charlesworth, R. (1997). Integrated developmentally appropriate curriculum: From theory and research to practice. In: C. Hart, D. Burts, & R.

Charlesworth (Eds.), *Integrated curriculum and developmentally appropriate practice: Birth to age eight* (pp. 1-27). Buffalo, NY: SUNY Press.

Hativa, N., Barak, R., & Simhi, E. (2001). Exemplary university teachers: Knowledge, and beliefs regarding effective teaching dimensions and strategies. *The Journal of Higher Education, 72,* 699-729.

Hendrick, J. (1997). *First steps toward teaching the Reggio way.* Upper Saddle River, NJ: Prentice Hall.

Hohmann, M., & Weikart, D. (2002). *Educating young children: Active learning practices for preschool and child care programs.* Ypsilanti, MI: High/Scope.

Howe, N., Jacobs, E., & Fiorentino, L. M. (2000). The curriculum. In: L. Prochner & N. Howe (Eds.), *Early childhood care and education in Canada.* Vancouver, British Columbia, Canada: University of British Columbia Press.

Howe, N., Jacobs, E., Vukelich, G., & Rechia, H. (2012). In-service professional development and constructivist curriculum: Effects on quality in child care, teacher beliefs, and interactions. *Alberta Journal of Educational Research, 57* (4), 353-378.

Howes, C., Burchinal, M., Pianta, R., Bryant, D., Early, D., Clifford, R. & Barbarin, O. (2008). Ready to learn? Children's pre-academic achievement in pre-kindergarten programs. *Early Childhood Research Quarterly, 23,* 27-50.

Jacobs, E., Vukelich, G., & Howe, N. (2007). *Pathways to constructivism: A self-directed guide for educators.* Montreal, QC: Concordia University.

Jalongo, M. R., Fennimore, B. S., Pattnaik, J., Laverick, D., Brewster, J., & Mutuku, M. (2004). Blended perspectives: A global vision for high-quality early childhood education. *Early Childhood Education Journal, 32,* 143-155.

Jalongo, M. R., & Isenberg, J. P. (2000). *Exploring your role: A practitioner's introduction to early childhood education.* Upper Saddle River, NJ: Merrill.

Johnston, S. (1996). What can we learn about teaching from our best university teachers? *Teaching in Higher Education, 1,* 213-225.

Jones, E., Evans, K., Rencken, S., Stringer, C., & Williams, M. (2001). *The lively kindergarten: Emergent curriculum in action*. Washington, DC: National Association for the Education of Young Children.

Jones E., & Nimmo J. (1994). *Emergent curriculum*. Washington, DC: National Association for the Education of Young Children.

Jones L., & Osgood, J. (2007). Mapping the fabricated identity of childminders: Pride and prejudice. *Contemporary Issues in Early Childhood, 8,* 289-300.

Kagan, D. (1992). Implications of research on teacher belief. *Educational Psychologist, 27,* 65-90.

Kagan, S., & Cohen, N. E. (1997). *Not by chance: Creating an early care and education system*. New Haven, CT: Bush Center in Child Development and Social Policy at Yale University.

Kamerman, S. (2000). Early childhood education and care: An overview of developments in the OECD countries. *International Journal of Educational Research, 33(1), 7-29.*

Kashin, D. (2009). *Reaching the top of the mountain: The impact of emergent curriculum on the practice and self-image of early childhood educators*. Koeln, Germany: Lambert Academic Publishing.

Katz, L. (1996). Child development knowledge and teacher preparation: Confronting assumptions. *Early Childhood Research Quarterly,* 11 (2), 135-146.

Katz, L. G. (1999). Balancing constructivist and instructivist curriculum goals in early childhood education. *Kindergarten Education: Theory, Research and Practice, 4,* 71-83.

Katz, L. G., & Chard, S. (2000). *Engaging children's minds: The project approach*. Norwood, NJ: Ablex Publishing.

Kontos, S., & Dunn, L. (1993). Caregiver practices and beliefs in child care varying in developmental appropriateness and quality. *Advances in Early Education and Day Care, 5,* 53-74.

Krough, S. L., & Slantz, K. L. (2008). *The early childhood curriculum.* New Jersey: Lawrence Erlbaum Associates Publishers.

Langford, R. (2008). Making a difference in the lives of young children: A critical analysis of a pedagogical discourse for motivating young women to become early childhood educators. *Canadian Journal of Education, 31,* 78-101.

Langford, R. (2010). *Innovations in provincial early learning curriculum frameworks* (Occasional Paper No. 24). Toronto, ON: Childcare Resource and Research Unit.

LaParo, K., Pianta, R., & Stuhlman, M. (2004). The classroom assessment scoring system: Findings from the pre-kindergarten year. *The Elementary School Journal, 104,* 410-426.

Lincoln, Y., S., & Guba, E., G. (2000). *Case study method.* London: Sage.

Maehl, W. H. (2000). *Lifelong learning at its best: Innovative practices in adult credit programs.* San Francisco, CA: Jossey-Bass.

Maccoby, E. E., & Lewis, C. C. (2003). Less day care or different day care? *Child Development, 74,* 1069-1075.

Manning-Morton, J. (2006). The personal is professional: Professionalism and the birth to threes practitioner. *Contemporary Issues in Early Childhood, 7,* 42-52.

Marcon, R. A. (1999). Differential impact of preschool models on development and early learning of inner-city children: A three-cohort study. *Developmental Psychology, 35,* 358-375.

Marcon, R. A. (2002). Moving up the grades: Relationship between preschool model and later school success. *Early Childhood Research and Practice, 4,* 1-25.

Marlowe, B. A., & Page, M. L. (1998). *Creating and sustaining the constructivist classroom.* Thousand Oaks, CA: Corwin Press.

Marshall, M. (1996). Sampling for qualitative research. *Family Practice, 13,* 522-526.

Maxwell, K., McWilliam, R., Hemmeter, M., Jones-Ault, M., & Schuster, J. (2001). Predictors of developmentally appropriate classroom practices in kindergarten through third grade. *Early Childhood Research Quarterly, 16,* 431-452.

McGillivray, G. (2008). Nannies, nursery nurses and early years professionals: Constructions of professional identity in the early years workforce in England. *European Early Childhood Education Research Journal, 16,* 242-254.

McMullen, M. B., & Alat, K. (2002). Education matters in the nurturing of the beliefs of preschool caregivers and teachers. *Early Childhood Research & Practice, 4(2),* 2-27.

McMullen, M. B., Elicker, J., Goetze, G., Huang, H., Lee, S., Mathers, C., Wen, X., Yang, H. (2006). Using collaborative assessment to examine the relationship between self-reported beliefs and the documentable practices of preschool teachers. *Early Childhood Education Journal, 34,* 81-91.

Ministry of Children and Youth Services. (2006). *Early learning for every child today: A framework for Ontario early childhood settings.* Queen's Printer for Ontario: Best Start Expert Panel on Early Learning.

Moss, P. (2006). Structures, understandings, and discourses: Possibilities for re-envisioning the early childhood worker. *Contemporary Issues in Early Childhood, 7,* 30-41.

National Research Council. (2001). *Eager to learn: Educating our preschoolers.* Washington, DC: National Academies Press.

Nelson, R. F. (2000). Personal and environmental factors that influence early childhood teachers' practices. *Journal of Instructional Psychology, 27,* 95.

New, R. S. (1999). What should children learn? Making choices and taking chances. *Early Childhood Research and Practice, 1,* 1-18.

Nias, J. (1989). Teaching and the self. In: M. L. Holly & C. S. McLoughlin (Eds.), *Perspective on teacher professional development* (pp. 151-171). London: Falmer Press.

Nimmo, J. & Park, S. (2009). Engaging early childhood teachers in the thinking and practice of inquiry: Collaborative research mentorship as a tool for shifting teacher identity. *Journal of Early Childhood Teacher Education, 30,* 93-104.

Nisbett, R., E., & Ross, L. (1980). *Human inference: Strategies and shortcomings on social judgment.* Englewood Cliffs: Prentice-Hall.

OECD. (2001). *Starting strong: Early childhood education and care.* Paris: OECD.

OECD Directorate for Education. (2004). *Early childhood care and education policy: Canada country note.* Retrieved from OECD website: http://www.oecd.org/dataoecd/42/34/33850725.pdf

Osgood, J. (2006a). Deconstructing professionalism in early childhood education: Resisting the regulatory gaze. *Contemporary Issues in Early Childhood, 7,* 5-14.

Osgood, J. (2006b). Professionalism and performativity: The feminist challenge facing early years practitioners. *Early Years, 26,* 187-199.

Pacini-Ketchabaw, V. (2005). The meanings embedded within childcare regulations: A historical analysis. *Contemporary Influences in Early Childhood, 6,* 41-53.

Pajares, M. F. (1992). Teachers's beliefs and educational research: Cleaning up a messy construct. *Review of Educational Research, 62,* 307-332.

Palinscar, A. S. (1998). Social constructivist perspectives on teaching and learning. *Annual Review of Psychology, 49,* 345-375.

Peisner-Feinberg, E. S., Burchinal, M. R., Clifford, R. M., Culkin, M. L., Howes, C., Kagan, S. L., & Yazeejian, N. (2001). The relation of preschool child-care quality to children's cognitive and social developmental trajectories through second grade. *Child Development, 72*(5), 1534-1553.

Perkins, D. (1999). The many faces of constructivism. *Educational Leadership, 57,* 6-11.

Phillips, D. C. (1995). The good, the bad, and the ugly: The many faces of constructivism. *Educational Researcher, 24,* 5-12.

Phillips, M. B., & Hatch, J. A. (2000). Practicing what we preach in teacher education. *Dimensions of Early Childhood, 28,* 24-30.

Phillipsen, L. C., Burchinal, M. R., Howes, C., & Cryer, D. (1997). The prediction of process quality from structural features of child-care. *Early Childhood Research Quarterly, 12,* 281-303.

Pianta, R., Howes, C., Burchinal, M., Bryant, D., Clifford, R., Early, D., & Barbarin, O. (2005). Features of pre-kindergarten programs, classrooms, and teachers: Do they predict observed classroom quality and child-teacher interactions? *Applied Developmental Science, 9,* 144-159.

Pianta, R., LaParo, K., & Hamre, B. (2008). *Classroom Assessment Scoring System (CLASS) Maual, Pre-K,* Maryland: Paul H. Brooks.

Porcino, A. & Verhoef, M. (2010). The use of mixed methods for therapeutic massage research. *International Journal of Therapeutic Massage & Body Works,* 3(1), 15-25.

Rafferty, A. M. (1996). *The politics of nursing knowledge.* New York, NY: Routledge.

Reynolds, C. (1996). Cultural scripts for teachers: Identities and their relation to workplace landscapes. In: M. Kompf, T. Boak, W. R. Bond, & D. Dworet (Eds.). *Changing research and practice: Teachers' professionalism, identities and knowledge.* London: Falmer Press.

Reynolds, A. J., Wang, M. C., & Walberg, H. J. (Eds.). (2003). *Early childhood programs for a new century.* Washington, DC: Child Welfare League of America.

Richardson, V. (2003). Pre-service teachers' beliefs. *Advances in Teacher Education,* 1-22.

Riley, D., & Roach, M. (2006). Helping teachers grow: Toward theory and practice of an emergent curriculum model of staff development, *Early Childhood Education Journal, 33,* 363-369.

Rinaldi, C., & Moss, P. (2004). What is Reggio? *Children in Europe, 6,* 2-3.

Roberts, S. (2000). Development of a positive professional identity: Liberating oneself from the oppressor within. *Advances in Nursing Science, 22,* 1-9.

Rushton, S., & Larkin, E. (2001). Shaping the learning environment: Connecting developmentally appropriate practices to brain research. *Early Childhood Education Journal, 29*(1), 25-33.

Salvage, J. (2006). More than a makeover is needed to improve nursing's image. *Journal of Advanced Nursing, 54,* 259-260.

Saracho, O., & Spodek, B. (Eds.). (2002). *Contemporary perspectives on early childhood curriculum.* New York, NY: Information Age Publishing.

Scarr, S. (1998). American child care today. *American Psychologist, 53,* 95-108.

Sheerer, M., Dettore, E., & Cyphers, J. (1996). Off with a theme: Emergent curriculum in action. *Early Childhood Education Journal, 24,* 99-102.

Smith, K., E. (1997). Student teachers' beliefs about developmentally appropriate practice: Pattern, stability and the influence of locus of control. *Early Childhood Research Quarterly, 8,* 221-243.

Snider, M., & Fu, V. (1990). The effects of specialized education and job experience on early childhood teacher's knowledge of developmentally appropriate practice. *Early Childhood Research Quarterly, 5,* 69-78.

Stacey, S. (2009). *Emergent curriculum in early childhood settings: From theory to practice.* St. Paul, MN: Redleaf Press.

Stipek, D., & Byler, P. (1997). Early childhood education teachers: Do they practice what they preach? *Early Childhood Research Quarterly, 12,* 305-325.

Stipek, D. J., Feiler, R., Byler, P., Ryan, R., Milburn, S., & Salmon, J. M. (1998). Good beginnings: What difference does the program make in preparing young children for school? *Journal of Applied Developmental Psychology, 19,* 41-65.

Strauss, A., & Corbin, J. (1998). *Basics of qualitative research: Grounded theory procedures and techniques.* Newbury Park, CA: Sage.

Sugrue, C. (1997). Student teachers' lay theories and teaching identities: Their implications for professional development. *European Journal of Teacher Education, 20,* 213-225.

Tatto, M. R. (1998). The influence of teacher education on teachers' beliefs about purposes of education, roles, and practice. *Journal of Teacher Education,* 49, 66-77.

Tickle, L. (2000). *Teacher induction: The way ahead.* Philadelphia, PA: Open University Press.

Tillema, H. H. (1995). Reflective dialogue in teams: A vehicle to support belief change in student teachers. *European Journal of Teacher Education, 20,* 283-296.

Twomey-Fosnot, C. (1996). *Constructivism: Theory, perspectives and practice.* New York, NY: Teachers College Press.

Vartuli, S. (1999). How early childhood teacher beliefs vary across grade level. *Early Childhood Education Quarterly, 14,* 489-514.

Vartuli , S., & Rohs, J. (2006). Conceptual organizers in early childhood content. *Early Childhood Education Journal,* 33(4), 231-237.

Volkmann, M., & Anderson, M. A. (1998). Creating professional identity: Dilemmas and metaphors of a first-year chemistry teacher. *Science Education, 82,* 293-310.

Whitebrook, M., Howes, C., & Phillips, D. A. (1990). *Who cares? Child care teachers and the quality of care in America. Final report: The National Child Care Staffing Study.* Oakland, CA: Child Care Employee Project.

Whitebrook, M., & Sakai, L. (2004). *By a thread: How child care centers hold on to teachers, how teachers build lasting careers.* Kalamazoo, MI: W.E. Upjohn Institute for Employment Research.

Whitty, P. (2009). Towards designing a postfoundational curriculum document. In L. Iannacci & P. Whitty (Eds.). *Early childhood curricula: Reconceptualist perspectives* (pp. 35-39). Calgary, AB: Detselig Enterprises.

177

Wilcox-Herzog, A. (2002). Is there a link between teachers' beliefs and behaviors? *Early Education and Development, 13,* 81-106.

Wilcox-Herzog, A., & Ward, S. (2004). Measuring teachers' perceived interactions with children: A tool for assessing beliefs and intentions. *Early Childhood Research and Practice, 6,* 1-16.

Woodrow, C. (2008). Discourses of professional identity in early childhood: Movements in Australia. *European Early Childhood Education Research Journal, 16,* 269-280.

Wood, E., & Bennett, N. (2000). Changing theories, changing practices: Exploring early childhood teachers' professional learning. *Teaching and Teacher Education, 16,* 635-647.

Zanting, A., Verloop, N., & Vermunt, J. (2001). Student teacher's beliefs about mentoring and learning to teach during teaching practice. *British Journal of Educational Psychology, 71* (1), 57-80.

Appendix A
Dear Centre Supervisor,

I am a graduate student enrolled in a PhD program at Concordia University (Montreal) currently living in the Kitchener-Waterloo area and working at Conestoga College. A requirement of my PhD program includes carrying out a research study that will add value to the field of early childhood education. As an individual who has worked in this field for 27 years, I have become interested in curriculum practices in Ontario child care centres. In order to carry out my investigation, I require your support for your centre to participate in this study, and in helping me recruit an early childhood educator from your centre.

I would like to take this opportunity to describe my plan for carrying out this study. The study includes a classroom observation of curriculum practices, and an educator interview. The classroom observation will be carried out by two individuals who are trained in this process. This should occur during a two-hour period of regular classroom activities. The educator interview will be carried out by me, at the child care centre, at a time when the educator is not working with the children. I would like to audio tape the interview for the sake of accuracy and retention of important details. During the interview the educator will be asked for curriculum documents that are used in the program, and for permission to take pictures of the physical environment of the classroom. These pictures will not include any children, staff, or distinguishing features of the centre.

Once you agree to your centre's participation in this study by signing a consent form and returning it to me, I will send you a sealed envelope containing information about the study to give to qualified staff working full-time in your preschool programs. Upon identifying participating educators, I will make arrangements directly with them to find a mutually convenient time for the classroom observation and the interview to take place.

The total length of time required to collect all data is approximately three and a half hours, (2-hour in-class observation and one- and a –half- hour interview).The interview should be conducted in a secluded location in the child care centre to allow for as little interruption as possible. Please be assured that it is my intention to collect all data for this study in a manner that is least disruptive to you and to your centre's functioning.

Please note that my study has received ethical approval from Concordia University and that all information collected through this study will be kept strictly confidential. No one other than I will have knowledge of the names of centres and individuals participating in the study. Actual centre names and participant names will not be used in any reporting of study results. Once I complete the study, I would be pleased to share group results with you and your staff in the form of a written executive summary.

I hope that you see how this study can contribute to advancing the field of early childhood education at this very exciting time and that you agree to your centre's participation. If you have any additional questions, please call me at (519) 748-5220 ext. 3393 or email me at gvukelich@conestogac.on.ca . If you are in agreement with your centre's participation in the study, please sign the attached consent form and fax to me at (519) 748-3505.

Thank you.
Goranka Vukelich

Appendix B

Dear Educator,

I am a graduate student enrolled in a PhD program at Concordia University (Montreal) currently living in the Kitchener-Waterloo area and working at Conestoga College. A requirement of my PhD program includes carrying out a research study that will add value to the field of early childhood education. As an individual who has worked in this field for 27 years, I have become interested in curriculum practices in Ontario child care centres.

I would like to take this opportunity to describe my plan for carrying out this study. The study includes a classroom observation of curriculum practices and an educator interview. The classroom observation will be carried out by two individuals who are trained in this process, during a two-hour period of regular classroom activities. The educator interview will be carried out by me, at the child care centre, at a time when you are not scheduled to be working with the children, and will be audio taped. During the interview you will be asked for curriculum documents that are used in the program, and for permission to take pictures of the physical environment of the classroom without any children or staff in the pictures.

Once you agree to your participation in this study by signing a consent form and returning it to me. I will contact you to find a mutually convenient time for the classroom observation and the interview to take place.

The total length of time required to collect all data is approximately three and a half hours (two hours for the in-class observation and one-and a –half hours for the interview. The interview time will be decided with you to meet centre scheduling requirements. Please be assured that it is my intention to collect all data for this study in a manner that is least disruptive to you and to your centre's functioning.

Please note that my study has received ethical approval from Concordia University and that all information collected through this study will be kept strictly confidential. No one other than I will have knowledge of the name of your centre or the name of the person from your centre participating in the study. Actual centre names and participant names will not be used in my dissertation or any publications that might arise from this study. Once I complete the study, I would be pleased to report group results to you and your Supervisor. This will be in the form of an executive summary.

I hope that you see how this study can contribute to advancing the field of early childhood education at this very exciting time and that you agree to participate. If you have any additional questions, please call me at (519) 748-5220 ext. 3393 or email me at gvukelich@conestogac.on.ca . If you agree to participate in the study, please sign the attached consent form and fax to me at (519) 748-3505.

Thank you

Goranka Vukelich

Appendix C
Classroom Assessment Scoring System (CLASS; Pianta, LaParo & Hamre, 2008)
Dimension Framework

Domain	Dimension	Indicator	Behavioral Observations
Emotional support	Positive climate	Relationships	Physical proximity, shared activities, peer assistance, matched affect, and social conversation
		Positive affect	Smiling, laughter, and enthusiasm
		Positive communication	Verbal communication, physical affection, and positive expectations
		Respect	Eye contact; warm, calm voice; respectful language; and cooperation and/or sharing
	Negative climate	Negative affect	Irritability, anger, harsh voice, peer aggression, and disconnected or escalating negativity
		Punitive control	Yelling, threats, physical control, and harsh punishment
		Sarcasm/disrespect	Sarcastic voice/statement, teasing, and humiliation
		Severe negativity	Victimization, bullying, and physical

		punishment
Teacher sensitivity	Awareness	Anticipates problems and plans appropriately, and notices lack of understanding and/or difficulties
	Responsiveness	Acknowledges emotions, provides comfort and assistance, and provides individualized support
	Addresses problems	Helps in an effective and timely manner and helps resolve problems
	Student comfort	Seeks support and guidance, freely participates, and takes risks
Regard for student perspective	Flexibility and student focus	Shows flexibility, incorporates students' ideas, and follows student leads
	Support for autonomy and leadership	Allows choice, allows students to lead lessons, and gives students responsibility
	Student expression	Encourages student talk, and elicits ideas and/or perspectives
	Restriction of movement	Allows movement and is not rigid
Classroom organization	Behavior management	
	Clear expectations behavior	Clear expectations, consistency, and clarity of rules

	Proactive	Anticipates problem behavior or escalation, low reactivity, and monitors
	Redirection of misbehavior	Effective reduction of misbehavior, attention to the positive, uses subtle cues to redirect, and efficient redirection
	Student behavior	Frequent compliance, and little aggression and defiance
Productivity	Maximizing learning time	Provision of activities, choice when finished, few disruptions, and effective completion of managerial tasks
	Routines	Students know what to do, clear instructions, and little wandering
	Transitions	Brief, explicit follow through, and learning opportunities within
	Preparation	Materials ready and accessible, and knows lessons
Instructional learning formats	Effective facilitation	Teacher involvement, effective questioning, and expanding children's involvement
	Variety of modalities and materials	Range of auditory, visual, and movement opportunities; interesting

			and creative materials: and hands-on opportunities
		Student interest	Active participation. listening. and focused attention
		Clarity of learning objectives	Advanced organizers and reorientation statements
Instructional support	Concept development	Analysis and reasoning	Why and/or how questions. problem solving. prediction/experimentation. classification/comparison. and evaluation
		Creating	Brainstorming, planning, and producing
		Integration	Connects concepts and integrates with previous knowledge
		Connections to the real world	Real-world applications and related to student lives
	Quality of feedback	Scaffolding	Hints and assistance
		Feedback loops	Back-and-forth exchanges. persistence by teacher. and follow-up questions
		Prompting through processes	Asks students to explain thinking. and queries responses and actions

	Providing information	Expansion, clarification, and specific feedback
	Encouragement and affirmation	Recognition, reinforcement, and student persistence
Language Modeling	Frequent conversations	Back-and-forth exchanges, contingent responding, and peer conversations
	Open-ended questions	Questions require more than a one-word response and students respond
	Repetition and extension	Repeats and extends/elaborates
	Self-and parallel talk	Maps own actions with language and maps students' actions with language
	Advanced language	Variety of words, and connected to familiar words and/or ideas
	Purposeful	Explains importance of print, and connects to or is embedded in real world applications

Appendix D
Early Childhood Educator Interview

Section 1: Demographic Information

1. Where did you receive your formal ECE education? _____College
   _____University
   _____Equivalency
   _____Through
   Apprenticeship

2. What year did you graduate with your ECE credential? _____

3. What is the highest post-secondary designation you have attained to date?
   <u>Designation</u>   <u>Area of Specialization</u>

   ___College Diploma   in   _____
   ___University Degree   in   _____
   ___Partial University Degree toward _____

4. How many years in total have you worked as a full-time early childhood educator?

   _____

5. How many years have you worked in this child care center as a full-time early childhood educator?

   _____

6. While working as an early childhood educator, have you attended professional development activities?

   _____ Yes_____ No

7. If Yes, please identify the activities which you attended during the last year, where they took place, how you chose to attend them, and who paid for your participation.

Professional development activity	How you came to choose to attend	Paid by

Section 2: Explanation of Observed Curriculum Practices

"As you remember _____ was here on _____ and observed you in your program. I would like to speak with you about some of those observations."

I will make reference to specific recorded observations and engage each participant in conversation. Through conversation, we will discuss the recorded observations by focusing on why various practices took place, various strategies that were initiated with children, and why educators responded in the way in which they did. The following are possible open-ended questions that I may use to guide our conversation:

- *"Can you tell me more about that incident (reference to recorded observations)?"*
- *"How did you come to decide to do that?"*
- *"Tell me about your intention in introducing or participating in that experience?"*
- *"Where did you learn to do that?"*
- *"I see that the children (make reference to observation), what do you think about that?"*
- *"I see that you (make reference to observation), why did you respond like that?"*
- *"Is that an important part of what you do? Why is that?"*
- *"How did the parents respond to (make reference to observation)?" How do you feel about that?"*
- *"Tell me about your room arrangement?" (inspiration for, and possible conditions for changes and why)*
- *"Can you practice in the way you want to?"*
- *"If Yes, describe supports in place that allow you to do that; if No, describe barriers that stand in your way."*

Curriculum Document to Collect

I will invite educators to provide me with relevant curriculum documents they are currently using, and that may have been referenced during the interview. The type of curriculum documents that may be collected include the following:

- Daily routine/schedule
- Samples of curriculum planning forms
- Samples of documentation panel formats
- Samples of child observation formats
- Samples of portfolio formats
- Samples of relevant curriculum policies

The conversation around the curriculum documents will focus on the following:

- *"Can you describe for me how you use _____?"*
- *"Can you tell me why you use _____?"*
- *"Tell me about the design and development of _____?"*

Section 3: Educator Beliefs

The conversation about beliefs will be inspired by the following guiding questions:

188

- How do you describe the curriculum in your program?
- How do you describe the most important role for curriculum in your program? Why?
- How do you describe the least important role for curriculum in your program? Why?
- Describe others' views about what you do as an educator. What are your thoughts about those views?
- Tell me what influences your ideas about the curriculum in your program.
- How do you communicate curriculum experiences that occur in your program?
- Who do you communicate these experiences to? Why?
- Describe the qualities needed to be an effective early childhood educator. Why?

"I am going to make 10 statements that are incomplete that I would like you to complete. There are no right or wrong answers. Just respond with the first thing that comes to mind."

1. The reason I became an early childhood educator is _____.

2. The most important aspects of my work as an early childhood educator are _____.

3. The least important aspects of my work as an early childhood educator are _____.

4. The most difficult aspects of my work as an early childhood educator are _____.

5. What excites me the most as an early childhood educator is _____.

6. What frustrates me the most as an early childhood educator is _____.

7. The parents of the children in my program view my work as _____.

8. The resources that I refer to most often in my work an early childhood educator are _____.

9. In my work as an early childhood educator, regulations _____.

10. People outside of the center view my work as _____.

11. If I were not an early childhood educator, I would be _____. Why? _____

Thank you very much for your participation.

Lightning Source UK Ltd.
Milton Keynes UK
UKOW01f1850291216
290994UK00001B/299/P